POACHERS CAUGHT!

Adventures of
a Northwoods
Game Warden

TOM CHAPIN

Illustrations by: HAL RIME

Adventure Publications
Cambridge, Minnesota

Illustrations by Hal Rime
Book design and typesetting: Mori Studio
Cover design: Mori Studio

Library of Congress Catalog Number: 2003110547

10

Poachers Caught!
Published by Adventure Publications
An imprint of AdventureKEEN
330 Garfield Street South
Cambridge, Minnesota 55008
(800) 678-7006
www.adventurepublications.net
Printed in U.S.A.
ISBN: 978-1-59193-206-2 (pbk.)

To Sandy

If deep down in your heart you are dishonest,

you can get around nearly any law—particularly a game law.

These game laws leave a man pretty much on his own.

Generally there isn't a game warden present.

So when you go afield, it's up to you.

Who'd know the difference?

You're all by yourself.

—*David M Newell*

November 1945

Table of Contents

Acknowledgments

Encouragement to write this book came from many directions including family members, friends and people from the community who have heard or witnessed the accounts on these pages. Hal and Winnie Rime, who have many tales of their own as former resort owners, have been nothing less than wonderful in their continued support throughout the entire process. Without brother-in-law Steve Koskovich assisting with the initial editing, I could not have withstood the rigors of transforming my thoughts into print. Then there's my father, Gaylord, who at 86, still shows his enthusiasm for my work as he did when he guided me through my early hunting and fishing years as a youngster. Finally, the one person in whom I am completely indebted, my wife of thirty-four years, Sandy, who has always shown confidence and support for my endeavors. Without her love and understanding this book could not have been written.

Introduction

A high score in the Outdoor category on my ninth grade career assessment inventory was no big revelation to me; woods and wildlife had fascinated me long before they merged into a vocation. Growing up with the natural world out the back door and encouraged by entrusting parents, my big desire as a teenager was to explore the "deep" forests and slog through swamps just to see what might be creeping around the other side. The day I was able to hunt alone with a shotgun became the catalyst for many future undertakings. Receiving a canoe for graduation also helped solidify my craving to "be outside" and pursue an outdoor occupation. By then if I wasn't fishing or hunting, I sure was thinking about it.

While many of my friends were engrossed in other adolescent pursuits, I was taking trips to the Boundary Waters Canoe Area Wilderness, bringing home wounded eagles or raising ducklings in the backyard. Snaring rabbits, trapping weasels, winter-spearing northern pike and dabbling in taxidermy took the remainder of my time. Tagging along with the local game warden and surviving a 42-below-zero overnight camping trip to cut deer browse (tree branches that deer eat for food in the winter) were some of the experiences that helped me decide to follow my passion in a wildlife profession.

The grind of the education years and surviving a two-year army stint made me appreciate even more the values of natural spaces and wild things. Now I poured everything into my quest. I passed the required testing and never looked back.

Who ever thought my experiences as a conservation officer would create a world far beyond my dreams as a green kid. The job, the events, the people—they have been nothing less than remarkable. What value can be put on the satisfaction a law enforcement officer receives when he knows, deep down, he has made a difference in a person's life. For example, the serious poacher, after being caught, who now teaches classes on hunter education. Or the stressed and stranded fisherman lost in a whiteout, saying thank you for his rescue. Also, creating an equal playing field for the sportsmen. For example, arresting a commercial minnow dealer who had made thousands of illegal dollars off public resources and was finally brought to justice. Or, after years of effort, finally catching a greedy couple with hundreds of fish belonging to the general public.

My decision to write this book was drawn from an assortment of motives. For years, immediately following each of my many slide presentations of fish and wildlife violations, I would invariably be asked, "Have you ever thought about writing a book?" "Those stories were great!" "You should get this stuff in print." I got the same reaction from my students during the past twelve years of teaching Natural Resource Enforcement classes at the local community college. "Best class I've ever taken so far . . . especially the stories and pictures." "If you ever decide to publish these, I want the first book!" These encouragements, along with the support and urging from my wife and friends, helped me decide to add this project to my list of retirement ventures.

I knew I had the resources to follow through. Besides writing a daily report, I had been a stickler on taking photos to help record the exciting and unique experiences of my twenty-nine-year career as a game warden. At the time, most were snapped for evidence, but as years passed, the value of these "stories in a picture" increased; they became my history. I discovered that the many accounts in my collection were also a great tool for getting the word out about poaching and for the promotion of ethics; I found I could make a difference.

Wildlife enforcement is really about fairness and equality. I always believed a game warden's job should focus on this one concern: providing an equal playing field for all who purchase a hunting or fishing license so that the legal sportsmen, regardless of income or political ties, aren't taken advantage of by the unscrupulous and greedy violator.

A game warden's job is unique compared to other types of law enforcement officers. Yes, we all take an oath to enforce and uphold the statutes, and we deal with much the same clients, but the methods by which conservation officers carry out their duties differ significantly. Other than traffic stops, much of a police officer's or sheriff deputy's duties involve investigation. However, most game and fish violations occur in a warden's presence. It's essential that a game warden put himself in a position to see the illegal shot, the extra line or the shined deer being loaded into the trunk, and this means, in many cases, working alone.

Conservation officers deal overwhelmingly with direct evidence. The officer is the witness. This one requirement is what makes the duties of a game warden so intriguing. Maneuvering into the correct spot and anticipating the detection of a poacher is sometimes as challenging and thrilling as the apprehension itself.

Finally, I hope these stories, as realistic and factual as my memory allows, will provide the reader with a heightened sense of appreciation for the over 6,000 wildlife officers in the country who are responsible for the protection of your fish and wildlife resources.

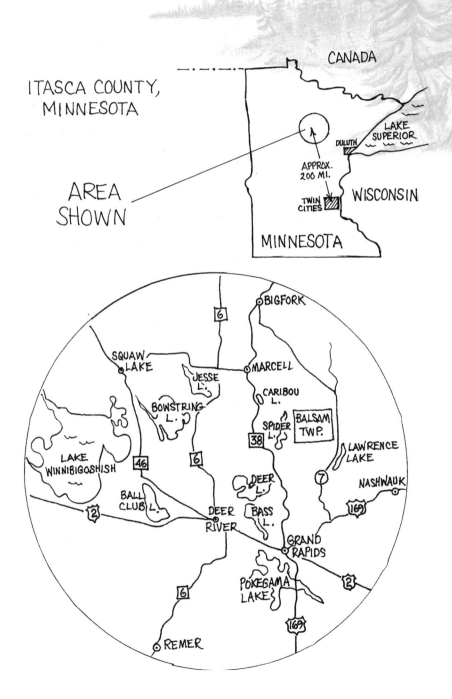

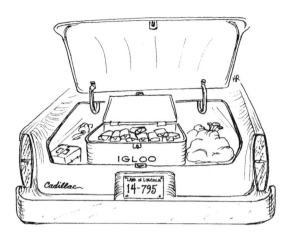

ONE

The Phony Figures

When a conservation officer's patrol area encompasses a large resort community, it is absolutely necessary to promote an open line of communication with the resort owners. They are the pulse of the fishing success and day-to-day activities on their own lakes. They have a wealth of information, so continued contact and interaction can be of enormous value when trying to identify the fish-poaching factions.

Communicating with resort owners can also be a huge challenge! They are in the business of making a living based on the return of their clients year after year. This is a delicate area for a conservation officer (C.O.) whose job is to ferret out the bad ones and discover their violations. That's why the education has to go both ways. The resort owner must learn as much as possible about the protection of a delicate resource that is the nucleus of his or her business, and the C.O. has the responsibility to listen to these owners about their needs and requests. With a mutual appreciation of each other's objectives, an officer can start identifying potential problem areas. Once these owners put trust in the relationship, positive things can start happening, as demonstrated by the following noteworthy case.

A resort owner team of husband and wife had been on my weekly schedule of stops over a couple of years for two reasons: They enjoyed the exchange of current information between themselves and a representative of the Natural Resource Department; also, their resort was in the heart of walleye country on a prolific fishing lake.

Most of the tips from resort owners are somewhat indirect. Many of the exchanges start with, "You might want to keep an eye on this guy" or "We have a couple that are leaving Saturday morning that may be of interest."

There is never anything specific, but the fact they picked up the phone to call means everything! Because of the relationship built up over the years, the resort owners came to trust me and knew that situations would be handled discreetly. Also I knew from experience that most owners wouldn't call on a violation unless it was a cut above the average infraction.

This call came during the middle of the week. According to the informant, an older couple from Illinois could be of interest to me. That was all. But it was enough to concentrate my work efforts the rest of the week on "this couple." I had also been furnished a general description of the man and the car he was driving.

Bowstring Lake, one of the larger lakes in the heart of Itasca County, is known for its excellent crappie and walleye populations as well as outstanding waterfowl hunting. It took a while, but on Wednesday morning I spotted the man trolling by himself on the south end of Bowstring. Approaching by boat, I detected three lines over the side, so it appeared he was angling with two more lines than the law allowed. A violation for sure but probably not the basis for the initial call from the resort owner. I figured talking to this guy was the only way to extract more evidence of other illegal activities.

Gripping the gunwales of his boat, I asked him to pull in the extra lines and show me his fishing license. A friendly sort of fellow, he totally complied and continued talking even after I advised him that a summons would be issued for the lines.

Trying my best to conceal my intent, I questioned him about his length of stay and his success so far during this beautiful week of weather. He declared the fishing to be generally poor during his visit and that his two weeks at the resort would end the next Saturday. Just looking at his equipment and fishing intensity and knowing that fishing had been excellent, I assumed at once that he was being deceptive.

At this point, I informed him of his options with the ticket and wished him a pleasant stay for the remainder of his vacation.

The next time we met was the following Saturday morning around 8:00 A.M. when a fellow officer and I stopped his 1998 white Cadillac heading south. "Oh, hi, you again!" he said. He and his wife appeared cordial, talking about the forty years they had patronized the same resort twice a season yet never having been checked by a warden during all those years. A large box of fish was in the trunk with each of 45 packages clearly marked with a number. Each number corresponded to a numbered list that the driver pulled from his pocket. He said that a list of fish caught accompanied every trip because he wanted to be legal and be able to show an officer just what he had in case he was ever stopped.

I checked the list with each package of frozen fillets and everything matched. The marked packages appeared to contain two full limits for him and his wife of walleyes, northern pike, crappies, bluegills, sunfish and other species of fish with large allowable limits such as perch and rock bass. The only problem was the fact that they were all frozen solid and virtually uncountable in this condition. The law allows fish to be transported in this condition only if they are packed by a licensed fish packer, which these weren't.

His apology for this inconvenience seemed completely genuine, and he was more than pleased to be on his way after receiving a summons for this minor violation. I seized one package of fish for evidence, just in case proof was needed that these fish were improperly packed and uncountable. Also, there were no one-inch patches of skin on the fillets for identification.

Well, this was another case based on an educated guess that found its way into the daily reports. I dismissed the whole stop as just another everyday enforcement activity. On to the next complaint!

After arriving at home in the early evening and throwing the package of fish in the sink for future inspection, I sat back and contemplated the day and direction it had taken. I was slightly frustrated after all the effort, but, hey, those folks were legal, and that was a good thing. Passing by the sink about 10:00 P.M., I noticed the package of fish that I had completely forgotten about. By then it was completely thawed, and the fillets could easily be counted and identified.

Ripping off the freezer paper, I separated the pieces and immediately saw walleye fillets; in fact, the whole package was walleyes! The writing on the paper declared only perch and rock bass, no walleyes. And they had at least 40 other pack-ages. I couldn't believe it. My feelings vacillated between anger, astonishment and finally despair. I knew there was nothing that could be done now. If I had only looked at the packages more thoroughly or questioned them further! I had a complaint from an excellent source. Why didn't I spend more time? All these thoughts clouded the whole event and soon I wound up questioning my own abilities. "Just put it away, Tom. Tomorrow's another day," I said to myself. Besides, this crew had forty years of experience. They'll be back next year. Yeah, but they got away from a couple of pro-fessionals who are paid to identify these things.

My mood didn't improve until I recalled a statement made by the driver that there was no way they could drive the entire distance back to their Chicago home and that an overnight stay was necessary. It was midnight, and I thought if ever there was a long shot, this was it. I thought, "Go for it, then I can get some sleep." I took a map from my glove compartment and drew a line from Bowstring, Minnesota, to Chicago, Illinois. I divided the mileage in half and found the closest town along the route home. Menomonie, Wisconsin, stood out clear on the map.

It was 12:30 A.M. when the Menomonie Police Department received my call asking them to assist me in checking out the motels in the area for a 1998 white Cadillac. They said, "No problem, we'll take a look right now." I was questioning my sanity for even involving them until the phone rang at 1:00 A.M. "Hey, warden," they said, "I think we found your white Caddy. It's parked in the Super 8 parking lot and matches the license number you gave us."

"Amazing! I owe you guys! One more favor. Have your local C.O. give me a call right away."

Ten minutes later, the local officer was on his way to the Super 8 to retrieve the fish at my request. The suspects were awakened and asked to turn over the fish to him for further inspection by the Minnesota officer they had met the day before. They were very accommodating and were told they could continue their trip home and that they would be contacted later after the outcome of the inspection.

I landed on Menomonee Lake the next morning, flown there by a C.O. pilot, Al. After meeting with the local C.O., we inspected all the packages and discovered at least 70 percent of the fish to be walleyes—more than 40 fish over the limit! I thought about all the years this had probably been going on and the potential fish that may have been poached over the last 40 years and 80 trips. That's a lot of resource that could have been available to other legal sportsmen on that lake!

The couple had the option of appearing in court or pleading guilty to the over-limit charges. Bail in the amount of $1,600 was posted the next week by mail and a guilty plea was accepted by the court. I believe they took care of it immediately because of the love of the area and the chance to return on future vacations. Due to his previous citation for using extra lines, he also lost his fishing privileges for a year.

The person convicted was very congenial during this whole episode. He appeared to be a very nice person who was overtaken by the greed factor after many years of never being checked. He even stopped at my office during the following summer to talk about his behavior and what it meant to him to finally get caught. He said that he just got carried away over the years with the quantity of fish that he was able to take home without ever being confronted. He said that he was legal the first couple of years, but the greed factor just took over, and after a while, the over-limits became routine.

If nothing else, this case proves the importance of an officer using visibility and a high profile, especially at resorts, as tools for deterring game and fish violations.

Minnesota Conservation Officer Pilot Al Buchert accepts the cooler of illegal fish with assistance from a Wisconsin warden.

TWO

The Humbling Hasp

Some episodes in a warden's career are unforgettable, others you try hard to forget. Owning a bagful of incidents I'd prefer to think never occurred, I recall two of the events that were especially awkward and extremely embarrassing. And both involved fish shelters!

Prior to 2003, an officer didn't need consent from the occupant to enter a fish house, dark house, fish shelter, portable shelter or spear house placed on public waters. The material used on these structures ranged from see-through plastic to corrugated metal skins. The majority of shelters in use today are portable cloth types with aluminum frames allowing easy set-up and maneuverability.

Quite a few years ago, I jumped on my snowmobile one mild sunny afternoon and headed for Trout Lake to check fishing success. It was a sparkling day that made the trip enjoyable. Bounding onto the lake crisscrossed with sled tracks, I aimed toward a group of shelters dotting the middle of a large bay. In another hour the sun would be setting over the trees ahead of me. This was the time of day most houses would be occupied.

I flipped the visor of my helmet all the way up to get a better look at the smoke puffing from the many fish house stoves. Without hesitation, I pulled up in front of a brown, hard-board-style house, turned off my machine, and walked to the door. "Game Warden. I'd like to check your fish," I hollered as I pulled the door open.

"C'mon in," was the response from two friendly gentlemen wearing hardhats. Apparently they came directly to the shelter after working a shift at the local mine.

Everything checked out and the final two minutes of our conversation included mostly the incidentals and successes of fishing. "Time to go," I said. "Gotta keep on truckin' to be home by dark."

As I exited the house and shut the door, I spotted a shiny object in the snow that turned out to be the padlock from the house. Casually picking it up, I hung it back on the wall and wished the two good luck.

After jumping back on my snowmobile, I pointed toward the next shack about 200 yards down the lake. Driving up and doing my usual approach, I met two people on their way out with a couple of speared northern pike in a bag. "Looks like you had some luck," I said as I peered into the gunnysack. "How long have you been out?"

"Couple hours at the most. It's been slow," they said as they ambled toward their truck. "What's going on over there?" one of them shouted as he pointed to the house from which I had just come. I glanced over and both men were performing some sort of labor, one on his knees and his partner bent over the doorway.

"I'll bet they just speared a big one," I said. "I'll run over and take a quick look." As I turned my machine around, I saw the two guys waving their arms at me to return. I signaled a "Be right there" motion, and zipped over.

"What's up? I suppose you speared a monster the minute I left. I've seen that happen a few times."

"Not exactly. You locked us in our house!!" exclaimed the one with a screwdriver in hand. Amazingly they didn't seem to be all that upset.

"I . . . I . . . did what?" I asked as I stood momentarily confused by the unexpected reply.

"Without thinking, you must have placed the lock over the hasp. We had to come out the side of the house!"

Instead of an opening where the door was attached, there was now a second cavity in the wall. Apparently the door's framework was too strong to overcome, so the two detainees had to escape through a hole punched in the weaker side-board.

I didn't have much to proclaim. Really, what could I say! Fourteen "I'm sorrys" didn't seem to relieve the tension. "Can I help with the repair?"

"No thank you. We think you've probably done enough," one of them mumbled.

After one more "sorry" and six "I'll certainly pay for the damage" apologies, I was back on the trail, a little more humble on the ride home.

While I was assisting my neighboring warden on Lake Winnibigoshish one cold morning, I skidded up to one of the countless dark houses scattered about the slick, frozen expanse. My snowmobile halted near the entrance, its engine idling as I disembarked and walked up to the door to identify my presence. "Game Warden . . . like to come in."

"Just a second . . . hold on . . . be right with ya," the garbled voice inside shot back.

"Open up. Let's see what you got," I yelled back.

"O.K. O.K. I've got to get the door."

So often, a person having something to conceal would delay the officer long enough to "clean things up." All doors on fish shelters must be built so they can be opened from the outside. I looked down and grabbed the oversized hasp jutting from the door frame and pulled. Nothing! I yanked. Still nothing! Assuming the door was locked from the inside, I took hold of the large hasp with both hands, my feet firmly braced against the wall, and jerked with everything I had.

It came this time! The whole door exploded off the hinges landing next to me now lying flat on my back. With one leap out of the gaping black hole pounced an enormous hulk of a dog. A yellow, slobbering mass of hair and drool landed on top of me, pinning me to the cold surface. As my life flashed before me, I tried some reverse psychology. "Hi, big guy. Are you friendly?" I said, trying not to reveal the terror gripping my supine form. The more I chatted, the more it licked. Luckily it was an even-tempered mutt!

I wasn't as sure about the owner's disposition. Yet to meet him, I manhandled the dog off me and slowly recovered my bearings and dignity as I returned to a standing posture, staring at the critter's owner.

Whoa, I thought, that was a demonstration of overkill. "Why was your door locked sir? What do you have in there you don't want me to see?"

"What do you mean what do I have in here? Nothing illegal! How come you tore my door off?"

"You weren't allowing access with your door locked, sir. I wanted in."

"All you had to do was turn the knob!!" he raged.

My face must have turned a pasty white at that insightful moment. "What knob?" I timidly murmured.

"This damn one right here!!" he shouted, as he rolled the now detached door on its side and pointed to a round one-inch diameter doorknob hidden behind the massive hasp. "See this one? It works fine," he reiterated as his hands demonstrated the proper method of operation.

My butt was in a wringer, and I knew it. All my energy was now directed into soothing his anger and making up for my aggressive blunder. I really had no excuse, so a request for forgiveness was now in order. I looked at the door and the shelter to which it was previously hinged. Just my luck, the entire structure looked brand new—all metal exterior with hidden rivets and a curved roof. "What can I do? Here, I'll help you with the repairs."

"No, I'll take care of it," he spouted back.

Maybe just conversing with him about other interests would help. So I sat on my snowmobile and talked and talked trying to direct his thoughts to more pleasant matters. Like where he was from (a town 30 miles to the west), and how many years had he been fishing this lake. A slight improvement in attitude began to surface, until after twenty minutes of shooting the bull, I figured it was time to make my getaway.

I started my snowmobile and slowly pulled away while wishing the man a final "Good luck" and offering a last apology. Finally I was in control, he appeared contented, and the situation seemed defused. One last wave over my shoulder—and one final shout from the fisherman over the engine noise: "ALL YOU HAD TO DO WAS TURN THE KNOB!!"

THREE

The Wrinkled Motorbike

In the early '80s, deer poaching in Itasca County, Minnesota, was peaking. Since the early '70s, when the deer population took a beating from several severe winters, the deer seasons had been very restrictive. They ranged from total closure in 1971, to picking an option of a three- or five-day season, to a more liberal nine-day season with almost a total ban on the taking of antlerless deer.

These restrictions and low deer numbers in Northern Minnesota caused a higher value and interest in putting venison on the table. Folks who made poaching a main hobby in the fall were now out in greater numbers doing their thing, even during daylight hours.

Itasca County in Northern Minnesota is blessed with remarkable resources including a multitude of small lakes surrounded by thousands of square miles of public lands. These areas, all open to hunting, include state, federal and county tracts in addition to many acres of private paper company and mining lands also open to outdoor activities.

Most rural landowners in the county have access to these parcels within a few miles of their residences if not straight out their back doors. To many, these are their favorite and most comfortable places to hunt.

In the lean years mentioned earlier, there were two townships that were especially notorious for the illegal taking of game and fish, especially deer. Both Lawrence and Balsam rural townships had the perfect environment of water, public woods and sparse population that generated a higher degree of game and fish lawlessness. This was confirmed by the records, by conversations with the previous conservation officers and by my own experiences in the previous eight years. At least half of my deer enforcement efforts during my first ten years were spent in just these two townships. This was significant considering they were only 10 percent of my total patrol district of 700 square miles.

In the middle of this section of land lived a very special person who provided me with a lot of information about hunting activity among the locals. This honest, direct-speaking lady, who is now deceased, hated poachers. They would harass her and her husband all year by continually shooting and taking animals on her pasture that bordered a tract of federal land for one-half mile. This prime deer spot was well known to the locals, with its main access going through the driveway of a resident known to take his own share of illegal animals.

I received correspondence from this sweet lady for almost seven years. She would write two-to-four-page letters describing illegal activities including the taking of two moose. She would also express in detail the peoples' relationships among their families and their neighbors. Her access to this information was a result of her work on the Bookmobile, picking up the local gossip, and the fact that party phone lines were still a form of communication at that time.

I received over 50 letters during those years all describing the Who's Who of a loosely knit poaching group. They would hunt mostly during the day and divide meat among the eight families or so involved. They did some hunting at night but mostly on foot due both to the increased chance of detection during night hunting and to the increase in shining cases being prosecuted in the county.

All her letters revealed an element of fear. Some of those folks considered hunting their total right, regardless of the laws, and nobody, including the local game warden, was going to stop them. Those feelings ran deep, and poaching was always a generational activity passed on to the younger family members. Law enforcement was the enemy. Her letters always ended with, "Please be careful, you're on their list." I always took this seriously and tried to stay as alert as possible, especially during night patrols. Having a fellow officer on board was valued during those times.

I would stop to see her about once a month to gather the latest information and to raise her confidence that someone was there to help her. Our meetings were always after dark and involved hiding my vehicle. She would not allow phone calls unless it was a total emergency. I could always detect some apprehension from her and her husband who were in their mid-seventies, just because I was there. As the years went by, she gained trust in me, especially after some of the culprits had been arrested. She would enlighten me as to what she heard after their arrests, which included more effort being put into avoiding law enforcement. Every meeting always ended in, "Please be careful, these are some bad boys." The following account is some of the information the lady provided over those years.

It was about six weeks before deer season on a warm, sunny day the last week of September. Fall Sundays in Minnesota are always big NFL days, especially when the Vikings are playing the Packers. I always tried to patrol at the places and during the times that the violators would least expect to see a law enforcement officer. What better time than during the middle of a Vikings game in a wooded area in Balsam Township!

Jumping on an old Honda 70 motorcycle, I headed into a heavily wooded area where a large power line held a sizeable deer herd. I headed north slowly on a one-lane grouse trail that was used both by walking hunters and hunting vehicles. This trail led to a maze of interconnecting paths linking the whole 30 square miles of prime hunting area. This tract was totally surrounded by county roads where some of these trails emerged. Mostly pine and fir trees bordered the trail as I continued north with sections of recently cut aspen dotting the hilly landscape. The periodic harvesting of these trees and the new growth it produced made this area very attractive to deer, grouse and other small game animals.

About a mile and a half into my Sunday afternoon patrolling venture, I saw a reflection ahead of me and noticed a vehicle approaching about a quarter mile up the road. I stopped my bike and waited for it to get closer when, at about 200 yards away, I recognized it as an older two-passenger army jeep containing two people. I could hear its engine and the tires hitting the bumps and puddles and making headway about as fast as it could considering the conditions.

To me, this would be a routine stop to check hunting activity, look at some licenses and make sure whatever firearms on board were cased and unloaded. The routineness suddenly came to an end when, at about 50 yards ahead of me, I could hear the engine pitch increase and saw the vehicle speed up toward me. Given the narrowness of the trail, the jeep couldn't get around me without driving into the brush. With only a second and a half to digest the situation and the vehicle only feet away, general fear and instinct kicked in. I jumped from the motorbike I was straddling at the time and landed in the brush along the trail. Looking up, I saw the jeep drive directly over the top of my poor little Honda.

The jeep continued south and disappeared around a corner of pine trees 50 yards down the roadway. "What the hell was that all about?" I said to myself as the initial shock started to wear off. I looked down the trail again, glanced at my twisted motorbike and thought, They can't get away with this.

Still shaking, less from fear than from the fact that those jokers were getting away, I ran to my bike and wondered if there was any possibility it would still function. Getting it up on its wheels, I found that the main damage was to the handlebars, which were twisted at 90 degrees with one handle sticking straight out to the front. I attempted to start the engine and listened to it cough and sputter until it started after five pulls. Well, let's go find these dudes and see what they're up to! I thought. I hoped they would take a right turn to the west which was a dead-end. If they went straight, I would lose them since they would connect with the main county road and be gone. Besides, I hadn't recognized the individuals—everything happened too fast.

Following the tracks in the moist dirt and fighting the handlebar challenge, I came to the fork in the road that determined their fate. "This is good!" They had turned right onto the dead-end. Next I wondered if they were that dumb or if they were setting up some sort of ambush. I knew the road only went about a mile and ended at a lake overlook. I made a decision to follow the track about half way and then skirt the edge of the woods in an attempt to identify someone or otherwise gather evidence to apprehend these folks. I stopped to listen for any noise ahead, but heard nothing.

As I got to within 50 yards of the end, I started to crawl through the underbrush to the little turnaround. This was the only place they could be as the other trails were too narrow to allow vehicle travel. As I looked up at the overlook, I could see the jeep with the passenger door and the tailgate open. I waited about ten minutes for any noise or conversation. After I was satisfied that nobody was around, I walked up to the back bumper and immediately saw the reason they didn't want to be checked out. There was blood all over the end-gate and pooled on the floor of the rear section. Down over the bank lay a young buck deer with entrails removed.

It was now the time to go get help. The keys were gone in the jeep so I pulled off some spark plug wires, got back to my bike and headed for the nearest residence. I phoned my fellow officer to the west who arrived in about an hour. We then drove to the site, took pictures and called for a wrecker. With the license plate at least telling us the owner's name, this case would probably come to an end quickly.

When the I.D. came back on the plate, I was not at all surprised. The jeep belonged to a person with whom I was all too familiar. Not that I had arrested him, but from the information I had from my little lady informant, I knew this was the ringleader of the poaching crew who had been taking deer for years. It was a Bingo day. I knew this guy enough to say "Hi" to him on the street, so maybe there was a chance to find out with whom he shared this illegal deed.

The interview over the phone about two hours later didn't take very long. They had both walked home about three miles from the incident through a lot of swamp and brush. I told him I was pretty upset about his behavior out there and his thinking that a deer was worth more than my safety and a motorbike. I eventually got him to the point of a little regret (mostly because he got caught) and I then told him to meet me at the Sheriff's office at 9:00 P.M. and to bring his partner with him. I told him that he was in some deep doo-doo and that bringing his buddy in might help his situation. It worked! At 9:00 P.M., there he was, coming up the steps, with his accomplice following close behind. I never thought there was really a chance to get #2, but there they were in all their poaching glory.

I conducted an interview and within two hours received signed statements from both as to their involvement in taking deer before season and assaulting a conservation officer. Court took place the following week with both men pleading guilty to poaching a deer and to assault. They were both given some pretty stiff fines for that time along with fifteen days in jail and revocation of their hunting privileges for three years. I also confiscated the jeep, in which he had just put a new engine. The last straw was the purchasing of his jeep at the state auction by a local attorney!

As the word spread that the main boys had been apprehended for, of all things, poaching a deer, and had to spend time in jail, the criminal poaching element had to regroup and change some of their methods of operation. Then there was a higher price on my head as verified through the letters of my lady informant. Not long after, her dog was found shot at the end of her driveway.

There is a very sad conclusion to this story. Two years later, my little lady's husband went out to his pasture on an autumn night after hearing shots fired on his property. He never returned! Three weeks of searching with dogs, planes and numerous search teams were unsuccessful. It has been twenty years. You decide!

The Jeep that was used as the assault vehicle while transporting an out-of-season deer.

FOUR

The Brassy Bruin

Wild animal complaints always took a lot of time in a conservation officer's schedule, but they were well worth the effort, if for nothing more than the amusement derived from some of the calls. One woman telephoned that her sister had a mouse running up her leg and she needed a "game warden" immediately! A young lady called early one morning to report that she needed my assistance to deal with a colony of salamanders found in her shower stall. A huffy individual called my neighboring officer one evening reporting she had almost hit a deer that jumped out in front of her car. She was upset that the deer's route was 100 feet in front of a "deer-crossing" sign. (I guess the Department of Natural Resources had failed to supply the deer with the proper reading skills to avoid these situations.)

One call stated that a wolverine (regardless of the fact that no wolverine has been seen in Minnesota since 1899) had been sitting in his pine tree all morning. He insisted that he was an authority on animal identification. (It turned out to be a porcupine.) Numerous calls about car-killed timber wolves almost always resulted in the discovery of a dead coyote or dog. A lakeshore owner frantically called about his full-grown German shepherd, which at the moment was being attacked by a pelican. He said he was going to shoot it if I wasn't out there immediately. I said that was O.K. as long as he didn't shoot the pelican. And finally, there was the call from a life-long rural resident that a fisher (8-pound member of the weasel family) was caught in a trap in his driveway, and he needed help in removing it. (It was a cub bear.)

Of all the animals that were the focus of complaints, however, black bears were the most notorious. Not only did the complaints drain off lots of time that could have been directed toward real enforcement work, but there was never an absolute solution other than destroying the animal or live-trapping it and depositing the nuisance in your neighboring officer's area. The average gripe would involve the bear scattering garbage around a yard, eating the dog's food, making pick-up sticks out of the bird feeder, or just the bear's menacing presence. There were very few of what I considered to be legitimate complaints. We'd advise the people to remove the attraction, but they'd retort that it was their right to have a yard resembling a landfill and that bird feeding was a God-given entitlement! The few legitimate complaints–destroying an orchard or a grain field, invading campgrounds or wandering around a schoolyard–were rare.

Another bear-related obsession: all bears are BIG!! They're like moose in that respect. Nobody sees a small moose. Same with bears. The public seems to know the difference between a bear cub and an adult, but all adults are BIG! Talking about seeing a medium size bear just doesn't grab the attention of your coffee buddies. I know this for a fact due to the thousands of bear stories I've heard over the years. (Bear stories are big things in small northern Minnesota towns.) I listened to so many bear tales that five years into my employment I put five dollars in my wallet and vowed to bestow it upon the first person who would say, "I saw a <u>small</u> bear!" I got through my whole career and a thousand bear reports with the moldy five dollars still in my billfold.

Working with bears in those days (currently Minnesota C.O.'s are no longer handling bear complaints) brought out some humorous and noteworthy incidents. Even though they appear intimidating, black bears are some of the calmest, most nonaggressive wild animals in the woods. They have very poor eyesight and are only attracted to one thing: food!

A call came in on a midsummer morning from a very anxious young lady. She had just returned home to her rural trailer house after two days away only to find that a bear had completely trashed the house's interior. Many times we could guess at the disorderly, sometimes garbage-strewn condition of the yard before we arrived. Her panicky voice suggested the bear might still be inside, but that was quashed after she said her father had come over and already checked out the damage. She said she had an eight-month-old baby, and there was no way she was going to re-enter her house until I arrived to check out the bear and possibly set a live trap.

The trailer looked like it had been backed into a swamp. Bears live in swamps, so conditions were perfect for some bear/human interaction. The yard looked like a critter feedlot with garbage strewn around the perimeter to serve as attractions for unwanted four-footed creatures. Dad and Uncle came over first to ponder the situation. Now they were a couple of interesting witnesses. One of them looked like a crusty Abraham Lincoln in overalls, and his partner, the uncle, appeared to be a shy, quiet, non-demonstrative sort of fellow. He just stood there repeating "Yup" to everything old "Abe" said, especially after Abe acknowledged that this destruction might have been the result of a BIG bear.

The young lady was almost beside herself with fear. I told her I would set a trap immediately and most likely the bear would be quickly caught. She calmed down slightly and then showed me the condition inside the trailer house. The bear had gone through the window and had come out the door. The window's glass was shattered inside the room while the entrance door was pushed to the outside. The bear was obviously attracted to a food odor, but amazingly, on the way out, it was unable to open the freezer full of meat that was sitting next to the entrance, although there were large tooth marks that had dented the exterior metal. Inspecting the tooth damage closer, I admitted to myself that this could have been caused by at least a not-so-small bear.

The inspection inside started at the living room end of the trailer. I couldn't believe the total and complete disarray, furniture tipped over and thrown everywhere. Every accessory that you could think of to a living area was on the floor: papers, toys, pictures, pots and pans, a vacuum cleaner. As I moved into the attached kitchen area, the mess got worse. Apparently the bear had an appetite for watermelon, as the rinds on the floor confirmed. The refrigerator door was wide open hanging on one hinge, and the refrigerator had very little food left inside. What was left of the perishables was on the floor or scattered around the counters combined with cans and bottles pulled from the cupboards. The floor was barely visible due to items covering most of the linoleum. The intruder apparently had also yet to be toilet trained.

Then came the hallway and the two adjoining bedrooms. I asked the shy young lady if I could take pictures of the destruction, and she gave me her permission. All she wanted was the bear to be gone and to not be a future threat. I took photos of the living room and kitchen, and as I waddled backwards stumbling over the debris, I focused the camera into the first bedroom. The room looked like a mini-tornado had twisted a path and deposited its rubble at random. Just after the flash went off, I felt a tug on my shirt. The young lady was trying to get my attention concerning the bedroom. She looked up at me and softly said, "Officer, the bear wasn't in here! Just thought you should know."

I looked at her, glanced back at the bedroom, looked back at her, paused, and said, "O.K. Maybe I'll just stop here and go outside to work on the trap."

As I stepped forward over the trailer's debris to get out, only one thought kept going through my mind: Just how much damage did the bear actually do? I had to totally reassess the actual mischief this bear had wrought. I honestly couldn't tell the difference between the bedroom's condition and the mess in the living room!

I put the culvert-style trap alongside the trailer and placed it so a snooping bear would easily enter and grab the bacon grease. Two hours later the lady called to tell me about the trap containing the biggest bear she'd ever seen.

Upon arriving, I discovered that she was right! It was a BIG bear. A huge black hulk of a hairy body was stuffed inside the culvert-type trap. It could barely move and was unable to turn around inside. The trap shook and shuddered as I approached. The bear's beady little red eyes strained to see through the wire mesh on the opposite end of the culvert. It would hiss and rake the wire with one of its fat front paws, simultaneously emitting a loud throaty growl that would cause you to jump out of your tracks.

This monster didn't appreciate his situation and wanted out! I told all the people gathered that this was undoubtedly the largest live black bear I had ever seen. The uncle exclaimed, "Yup, I believe so!" I asked him if he wanted a closer look. He slowly approached the wire-meshed guard on the front of the cage, and just as he put his nose up to the wire to take a quick peek, WHAM, the bear hit the inside with full bruin force, spitting a sleek gob of bear saliva directly into his face.

I always had asked folks if they wanted a closer look and every time, wham, splat, and a loud shriek. Until their hearts got started again, most were pretty speechless. (I always thought I should stop doing that, but it was just too much fun. I thought it was a chance, for those interested, to truly interact with some of our wildlife.)

I quickly attached the trailer and drove the big 600-pound creature to a remote public site 20 miles north of town where I released it.

About a week later, I received a note from the young lady thanking me for taking care of her bear problem and wishing me well. (Nothing on the card from her uncle, the recipient of bear spit.) To this day, she remains high on my list of special people. The young lady's harsh living conditions didn't lessen her capacity for a tender heart. Her letter is the only thank you note I've ever received after a career of removing over 200 nuisance bears.

This is what a 600-pound black bear can do when it ransacks a trailer house.

FIVE

The Right Spot at the Wrong Time

More licenses are sold for the sport of fishing than for any other outdoor pursuit, and no other leisure interest includes such a wide range of ages and professions among the population. There are a million and a half fishing licenses sold just in Minnesota, and in many areas of the state the fishing is better than it was thirty years ago. Much of this increase in productivity has to do with the way the resource is managed and the improvements in scientific knowledge in terms of sustainable fish management of each species as it is applied to each lake type.

The main tools used by these managers, of course, are the laws and regulations that restrict the number of fish that one can possess and the methods by which they are taken. The fish species most sought after is still the walleye, followed by some of the panfish varieties, such as the crappie.

All 140 or so conservation officers in the state have some degree of fishing in their patrol areas, and to some, it is their primary enforcement challenge. In Itasca and neighboring Cass Counties, the biggest walleye factory is 58,000-acre Lake Winnibigoshish or just "Winnie" to the locals. This lake has experienced some off-years of fishing, but over the long haul it's been a mass producer of excellent walleye and northern pike. Recently, a length limit has been introduced on the lake, which should improve the fish size and productivity just that much more.

Enforcement work on this huge body of water has afforded some fascinating interactions and experiences. Combine the 12 resorts, numerous public and private campgrounds and a large angler turnover once a week, and the lake becomes a real challenge in trying to maintain an equal opportunity resource. The vast majority of folks who come here, many from other states, totally appreciate the natural beauty of the lake and its surrounding national forest borders and the bountiful treasures below its surface. For the most part these folks are also law abiding and support the enforcement activities that help protect the very resource that draws them and their money to the area.

However, when this many people are gathered to recreate at one time, there are bound to be those who will take advantage of the system. This small percentage of violators reduces the resource available to the legal anglers and eventually affects everybody to some degree. The success of effective patrolling in an area this big is directly related to the visibility of an officer and the relationship the officer has with the commercial resorts. If citizens know that there is a chance of being caught for their infractions, in most cases they will change their behavior. And that's what it's all about in game and fish enforcement—changing the conduct of those who might bend the laws in order to satisfy their greedy intentions. This is not as easy a job as you would assume since it's fairly easy to hide a fish or a bag of fillets. In most cases, without help from the public, enforcement is almost impossible.

A call came in one Sunday morning from an angler reporting two people in a blue boat with Wisconsin registration who were double-tripping. This is the taking of a full limit of fish, returning to a location and dropping them off, and then catching and keeping another limit in the same day. He also followed the boat to the vicinity of their cabin, identifying a van with

Wisconsin plates parked in the driveway. In Minnesota and most states, a person can legally possess only one limit of fish at any time no matter where they are kept. Without a witness, this is the most difficult violation to observe as an officer.

It was late afternoon by the time circumstances allowed me to arrive at the sheltered lagoon area where many cabins and trailer houses border the water's edge with its connecting boat docks. According to the information, the potential violators were in the third or fourth trailer house from the end, and the van would be parked on the left side of the porch area. At the fourth trailer I spied the van with Wisconsin plates and no other vehicles within two houses either way. After knocking on the door and identifying myself, an older gentleman let me in after I explained the complaint I'd received. He graciously gave permission to look in his kitchen freezer where there were 20 walleye fillets—four under their limit.

As I looked back over my shoulder, I noticed the man's wife frantically removing packages from another freezer on the porch I had just walked by. I walked to her and asked what she was doing and there was no response. I leaned down and picked up a package that appeared to be partially frozen fillets. Asking again what this was, and again getting no response, I opened it. It was all walleye fillets, and there were many more packages. Finally forced to be a little more direct in my intentions, I told the lady that these would also have to be examined. After giving me a bewildered look, she allowed me to step in and remove all the fish. They totaled another 52 fillets. Adding the initial fish from the kitchen freezer, there were over 36 walleyes in possession, at least 24 over their legal limit.

After some discussion with both of the occupants, I told the gentleman I would like to inspect his boat knowing that the older blue craft might also contain more fish. He led me down the shore to the dock where there were five moored boats. He immediately jumped into a newer white and red boat, opened the back live well compartments, and said, "Take a look. There's nothing in here."

"Hold on a second—this is your boat?"

"Yup," he said, "I keep it here most of the summer."

Dumbfounded, I checked out the live wells and some other compartments and found nothing. Then I asked, "Do you know who owns this blue boat over here?"

"Oh yeah, that belongs to our neighbor next door, but they left about an hour ago!"

"Do you know if they were out fishing this morning?"

"Yes," he said. "They were out all morning and came in early this afternoon."

I then checked out the blue boat and found nothing but a couple of fresh minnows still on the bottom of a bait bucket.

After further discussion with this man, the obvious conclusion was this: The information from the tip had nothing to do with the cabin I actually searched containing the over-limit of fish. In other words, the wrong van was spotted, the wrong cabin was checked and two non-suspect people were guilty and arrested as a result. This whole situation was random, which is very disturbing. If an officer can arbitrarily pick out a cabin and, with no indication that there is a violation, find illegal goods, then one has to reassess just how much of this type of activity might be actually taking place.

SIX

The Incriminating Deer Head

T he deer seasons have always been crazy times for a conservation officer. Deer season in Minnesota is an estab-
lished institution with its traditions and rituals
unmatched in any outdoor sport. To many, opening weekend is
a holiday from the doldrums and monotony of their everyday
obligations. The enthusiasm in pursuing the wily whitetail can
be an obsession with some folks. This craze to possess a deer at
any cost is where enforcement sometimes becomes involved.
This passion to fill a tag many times translates into behavior
that falls outside the law. Many violators probably wouldn't
break any other laws, but when it comes to game laws, they're
caught up in the adventure. I've always had a soft spot for
hunters who sometimes got carried away with their eagerness.
After all, it's a gratifying, exciting time and a wonderful escape,
an experience I also enjoy, as long as the limits and safety laws
are followed.

One sunny opening morning south of Grand Rapids, my
fellow officer to the east and I were patrolling a large tract of
paper company land for illegal taking of fawns and does. That

particular year, permits to take antlerless deer were at a minimum. Many times does and fawns would be taken and transported without tags or left in the woods to be tagged later. We both saw a hunter dragging a deer toward the road on which we were traveling and stopped to check out his license and tag. The gentleman appeared a little surprised to see us but was hospitable enough for small talk and a license inspection. The deer was tagged, but being a small buck fawn, it required a special antlerless permit. That's when the attitude did a 180. "What do you mean I need a permit? Can't you see that's a buck?"

"It's definitely a male deer, Sir, but it's a fawn and doesn't come close to meeting the requirements of a buck deer with 3-inch antlers."

"What do you mean no antlers?" said this very large, tall man with a gruff exterior. "I could see them through my scope 150 yards away." Sometimes, even with the experience that we accumulate about body language and demeanor, you still don't know where a person's coming from when they're put in a difficult position. The hunter was telling us that his deer, lying there with no antlers, just nubbins below the skin, had antlers visible at 150 yards. Arguing about such an obvious thing isn't going to settle anything, so you just say, "Here's your ticket. Tell it to the judge."

The courtroom on Monday morning was packed with a row of people standing along the back wall. Many were there to enter either a guilty or not guilty plea to their game violation summons. I finally found a seat in the back next to a deputy and waited for my man to be called up. In those days the judges liked to have the officers present. This would help them make a better decision on the penalty if a plea was guilty, especially if there were extenuating circumstances.

Finally my tall gentleman violator was called forward to the judge's bench, and the first mistake he made was to lean both his elbows on the edge of the bench. Either he was unaware that this was sacred ground or he just possessed some bad manners, but the judge immediately let him know that he had transgressed the rules of courtroom etiquette. I thought, this is going our way already and nothing has even been said yet!

The courtroom was still full of people waiting their turn when the judge asked the man's plea. Guilty or not guilty? "Well, I'm not sure what I want to do. I want to tell my story and how I was treated by the officers." The judge held his ground and said that he needed a plea before he would let him discuss the case. That didn't seem to deter Mr. Tall as he continued to let his mouth run amuck. He blurted out that he shot a legal deer and it had antlers and the officers were wrong in even stopping him. The frustrated judge finally asked if the officer was present and if so would he approach the bench and straighten this out. I was more than happy to accommodate as I assumed this guy was going to make a fool of himself, and besides, I had done my homework. Clutching a paper bag, I walked up the crowded isle and asked the judge if he would like to see the particular deer in question. He said, "You bet I would."

"May I lay it on your bench, Your Honor?"

"You may Officer." The judge slowly opened the bag and there in all its antlerlessness was the deer head from the illegally taken fawn. "You say there are antlers, sir. I can't even see the damn things from here! I find you guilty, and the fine of $300 will be doubled due to the attitude that you've displayed in this courtroom. Next case!"

Mr. Perpetrator suddenly exhibited a reversal in his posture and general attitude. He turned around with stooped shoulders and meekly walked the length of the aisle to the back door of the courtroom. It was over, but my sense of satisfaction didn't last long when I picked up the bag containing the deer head, for underneath was a large pool of bright red blood—on the bench where the judge wouldn't allow a finger. "Sorry, your Honor," I said.

"No problem, Officer. Be careful out there," he replied.

As I turned to leave, I then noticed a trail of blood all the way down the aisle to the back of the courtroom where I had been seated. Due to the heat, the head had warmed enough in the courtroom to allow the flow of blood through the bag. I walked out, proud of thinking to bring in the head for evidence, but a little embarrassed that I didn't do a better packaging job!

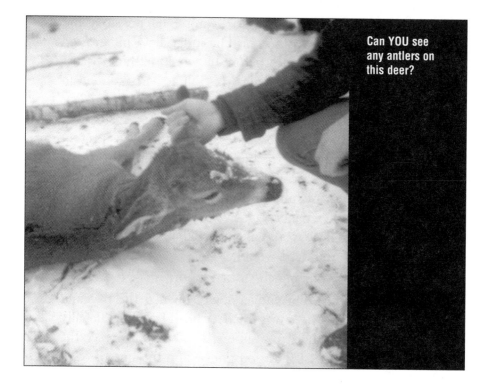

Can YOU see any antlers on this deer?

SEVEN

The Stealth Lights

The spring fish run has always been one of the peak times of the year for long hours and overtime in conservation enforcement work. Safeguarding the breeding populations in the spring is a valuable tool of fish and wildlife managers. As the snow melts and the ice recedes from the shoreline, most species of fish are heading to their annual haunts to spawn and generate their offspring.

This is also the period when fish become most vulnerable and surrender all their natural defenses. Prior to spawning, fish in lakes start to migrate to the shallow areas of these bodies of water and toward the faster moving flow of the incoming creeks and rivers.

Each species varies in their needs for time, water temperature and bottom conditions during spawning, but generally the "run" for each group never lasts more than two weeks. This shallow water spawning allows the unscrupulous fish poacher to do a tremendous amount of damage to the local fish populations by removing healthy, prolific adult fish. These folks know the locations of these highly productive locales and many times this information is passed on down through generations. The methods used include spears, dip nets, gill nets, firearms, traps, snagging, and even taking by hand. Removing fish in these ways is considered very unethical among the legitimate sportsmen and is becoming less socially acceptable even among the hardcore poaching factions.

Spring fish poaching has become less of a threat to the resource in Minnesota since the early '90s due to the higher penalties being imposed. Also, formerly remote areas that once were hot spots for this kind of activity are much more populated. The '70s and '80s in Itasca County afforded some very interesting episodes for conservation officers.

A particularly infamous spot north of Grand Rapids had eluded enforcement for years. One of the reasons was the difficulty in getting access to the creek because of the private land surrounding both sides, as well as the homes that were situated near the roads bordering the land. Another reason was the lack of information about the time of night and the particular days the illegal acts were taking place.

Most fish poaching in the spring takes place during the dark hours. That's when the fish run in the heaviest concentrations and detection is less of a concern for the poacher. Since I had help from a fellow officer this particular night, we decided to wait until well after dark and walk in about a mile to a spot about which I had previous information over the years. Avoiding the farmhouses and sneaking through a 40-acre field and into a patch of woods, we both stopped to rest and listen.

It was one of those new moon evenings at midnight—totally dark and still—and just above freezing. We were close enough to the creek that we could hear the faint sound of moving water. Knowing there was a small one-man bridge nearby, we crept in that direction and stopped again about 40 yards from the bank to wait out the rest of the night. We'd take a chance that this would be the spot poachers might pick because of the bridge and its deserted location.

After sitting for about a half hour, we both heard it at the same moment, a slapping noise just above the almost imperceptible swish of the moving water. Softly I said to my partner, "What do you think?" He shared the same feeling for what it might be. Slap! There it was again! We both twisted around in the direction and in the total darkness could see nothing. Of course, there had to be some form of light if this noise was indeed man-made, but nothing. "We have to get closer," I said, "because you and I both know that was the sound of a large fish striking the ground."

Our expectations rose as we slowly crawled that 40 yards through the brush to the bank's edge. We still couldn't see anything and we were right above the bridge. There it was again. Slap! And it was close, right on the other side of the 20-foot bridge. Then, after concentrating on the area for about two minutes, I noticed some sort of faint movement on the bridge. There was just enough starlight to confirm a slight motion. If someone was taking fish, how could they do it with absolutely no light? Whispering our next move, we decided to "rush the bridge," just like in the movies. We stumbled as far down the slight embankment as possible without our flashlights turned on, and then almost at the bridge's edge, we hit them!

What we experienced next was instant mayhem, with three persons scattering in every direction. We didn't have the best odds, but in their desperation, two of them made a huge mistake—they ran right in our direction. Both of them got around us and tried climbing the bank, but a couple mighty fine tackles ended their escape. My partner held them both as I ran across the bridge in an attempt to capture the third party, but he had just enough time to slide into the darkness of the woods and disappear. Running back to our two captives I wondered, Why did they run and what's really going on here?

Next, we secured the two men and advised them that they were not under arrest but only being detained until we got some more information to explain what we just witnessed. That didn't take long! Lying on the ground at the other end of the bridge were four beautiful, large, shiny northern pike; on the bridge was a long-handled spear. This looked like the crew that I'd received complaints on over the years, but how did they spear fish in the dark?

Looking over the edge of the bridge, which was three feet over the surface of the water, I saw some light being emitted from the sand bottom of the river about three feet deep. In fact, there were two lights. Taking the spear and reaching down, I collected both sources of illumination: two flashlights sealed in plastic bags. Fish are attracted to any light source, and these bags were positioned on the bottom of the river facing downstream. Since most fish travel upstream to spawn, these pike would see the light and nose themselves right up to the head of the flashlight and then, wham, another fat northern for dinner. These little tricks don't come naturally; most likely they're handed down through the family and the neighborhood where this type of illegal activity has gone on for generations.

Knowing these two guys would be appearing in court the next week, I asked the judge for an innovative sentence that might help send a message around the block. The judge agreed for the two to pay no fine but rather to spend a full weekend picking up trash and garbage at the public accesses in the area. That weekend happened to be, by no mistake, the opening weekend of fishing season.

EIGHT

The Dropping Duck

The modern era of duck hunting in America began when centuries of uncontrolled commercial waterfowl harvest led to the enactment of the Federal Migratory Bird Treaty Act in 1918, that banned their sale and imposed limits and other restrictions. Strictly a sport today, duck hunting is on every game warden's working agenda, a duty not easily accomplished given the great amount of time required to check compliance on a small number of hunters.

Since ducks migrate across borders, their taking is controlled by both state and federal regulations—state wardens having authority to enforce each. The methods of taking waterfowl and daily limits differ to some extent between states; nonetheless, most migratory waterfowl hunting in this country is under the same general restrictions. These restrictions include the chasing and taking with a motorized vehicle, hunting in open water without vegetation cover, and using a shotgun not capable of holding more than three shells. Most hunters comply with the mix of rules, particularly when accompanied by their children who need to learn early the "right way" to conduct themselves in the blind.

Two weeks before season a few years ago, I was searching out a good "duck spot" to work on the morning of the upcoming Opening Day. I came upon a fresh campsite near a small lake just north of Lake Winnibigoshish. It appeared to be set up for the arrival of a future hunting party. The remote, hour-glass-shaped lake was situated a mile off the beaten path with only a walking trail leading to the access site—a perfect spot for preseason surveillance.

Prior to sunrise on opening morning, a neighboring officer from the Leech Lake Indian Reservation and I approached the camp and hunkered down in a brushy area near the lake to await the noon start. Outfitted with binoculars and patience, we observed movement between the tents and the water—seven men loading boats, organizing guns and decoys and repairing blinds along the shore.

Because they were hunting in such an isolated area, it was unusual that we did not witness violations of early decoy placing or shooting prior to noon. This crew appeared to be following the regulations as the first ducks were shot about 12:10 P.M.

My plan now was to hike a mile cross-country to an adjacent lake where we had heard heavy shooting at 11:00 A.M., an hour before the season opened. We would return here later in the afternoon to check bags, guns and licenses.

As we packed up for the walk, I took one last glance across the lake through my binoculars, . . . a glimpse of a boat in motion in the direction of most of the shooting. The heat waves rising from the warming water, combined with the extreme distance, made it difficult to distinguish more than two blurred camouflaged figures. A short time later I caught the glint of a gun barrel pointed out the side of the motorized craft. Then, BOOM . . . BOOM . . . two reports from the shotgun out of the bow of the boat. They were motor-boating ducks!

For the next hour, back and forth they would skip across the end of the lake, racing into the flocks of Ringnecks and slaying them from the boat. BOOM!! Another duck would tumble from the sky and splash ahead of them. We were hard-pressed to take action; we could only watch intently and scribble notes until we could confront them back at camp later in the day.

About 2:00 P.M., a second boat that had not been visible, approached us from the north section of the lake. As it passed through the narrows about 100 feet away, I saw a man in a short-sleeved shirt with a shotgun lying across his lap operating his six-horse outboard at full throttle. As we split up to get a closer look, I crawled to the edge of the water and crouched behind a clump of cattails. The boat ran directly down the middle of the lake and met up with the other two hunters on the water. During this time, three additional members had arrived back at camp and were moving behind me between blinds. I was unable to move at all for fear of being spotted—I was only five feet from the trail that was continually being used.

Ten minutes later, the single-occupant boat returned in my direction while at the same time the crunching steps of two others passed within four feet of my ground-hugging body. Why they didn't see me, I'll never know. They must have been focused on the guy in the boat who now started shooting. I sneaked a quick look from my stomach position to make out the operator holding his shotgun directly over his head, and at full speed, blast a duck out of the air. As the ball of feathers plummeted closer, I actually covered my head for fear it might hit me. The fat mallard landed with a big THWOP 20 feet down the beach.

At that moment, the two guys who had just passed behind me yelled, "WAY TO GO, WEEZER!" At least now I had a name. Good old "Weezer" was added to my list of suspects in company with the two who were still harassing ducks to the south. KERPOW! Weezer shot at another fowl but missed his target. "GO WEEZER, GO!" . . . more encouragement from his buddies standing 30 feet to my left.

Weezer pursued his illegal antics for another fifteen minutes, busting another duck as he straffed the bulrushes along the opposite shore. Now everyone in the group was roaring encouragement to Weezer from the blinds and boats surrounding the little lake. Congratulatory whistles and expletives echoed his exceptional ability to run down and dispatch ducks from a motorboat. It had turned into a circus atmosphere as the other boat drew nearer our position. Meanwhile, we lay motionless in the brown grass, adamant in our desire to collect more evidence.

We had fingered five of the seven cohorts on various taking and transporting infractions before the whole team suspended their escapades and gathered at the camp access.

Our intention was to make our presence known only when all the members were grouped in a cluster. If any had an inclination to leave the scene, approaching them as a bunch might reduce the odds of escape.

After crawling up to the perimeter of the launch site, we stood up 20 feet away and just walked toward the whole bunch. Two of them noticed us immediately and turned to walk away. "Hold on there a second. Game wardens! We'd like to talk to everybody at the same time. C'mon back here. C'MON BACK HERE!!"

They turned in our direction and ambled back to the group.

I began, "How about everybody sit down and relax while I explain our intentions? We've been watching your hunting behavior since early this morning, and we'll be discussing our observations. First, why doesn't everybody pull out their I.D.'s, hunting licenses and duck stamps for inspection."

It became apparent during the subsequent interview that this was a good bunch of guys. Friendly and cooperative, the chit-chat turned into a learning experience for both sides. They were educated on the finer points of legal duck hunting, and we discovered this was the second generation of hunters who secured this campsite on opening day every year – and they had never been checked by a warden in thirty years! "We just got sloppy with the rules after all these years. It's probably a good thing you caught us. Otherwise, we would have gotten much worse," one of them added.

As I looked over the whole crowd, I gestured toward one of the more stout members and said, "Would you happen to be 'Weezer?'"

Sporting a shy, proud smile he growled, "Yup. That's me!"

The others chimed in, "That's our Weez. That's the Weez-man!"

"That's what I thought. Maybe I'll talk to you first."

We all had a good laugh with the affable Weezer, now the center of attention.

Only a few had proper licenses. Four were charged with transporting loaded firearms in a motor vehicle. Three were issued tickets for taking migratory waterfowl from a motorboat and two for possession of lead shot. One shotgun was confiscated.

They eventually thanked us for a couple of warnings afforded them and declared, "I think we've learned our lesson. You won't have to worry about this place anymore."

I believed them! This case also reaffirmed an axiom of enforcement work—C.O. visibility is one of the most important factors in deterring wildlife violations.

NINE

The Sunken Stringer

Itasca County overflows with first-rate fishing hot spots. It was always a challenge trying to guess which location would attract the most fishing activity on the night before season. There were always those who desired to "get the edge" on the legal fishermen by angling a few hours prior to the midnight opener, kind of like taking "cuts" in line.

One wacky event involved some fishing that was taking place on a popular local body of water. This prime fishing hole is called the "hot pond" due to the warm water that is discharged from a nearby electric power plant. The hot water eventually flows into the Mississippi River, resulting in many species of fish being drawn upstream into this small round lagoon.

Considering it was early May, this particular calm Friday night at 50 degrees was unusually warm, with a dark, overcast sky hanging above the little fish-pool. Many people would flock to this site hours before the midnight opener to secure a good position. The largest fish concentrations would be directly in front of the discharge culvert where the boat and shore fishermen shared the two acres of water.

My interest was in fisherpersons who would jump the gun and keep fish two to three hours before the official midnight opener. The only means to approach the hot pond was to walk a quarter mile along a fence that led to a slight rise overlooking the entire surroundings. Using the total darkness for cover, a friend and I took a position in some tall grass just above the marshy shoreline. Even using the binoculars, it was impossible to tell exactly how many boats were anchored in the little bay. The sound of people talking and the clanking of equipment were the only indicators of human activity.

As we sat and listened, I spotted a faint, almost indistinguishable light being emitted from the middle of the pond. Focusing in with the binoculars, it appeared to be a very small flashlight that would emit a glow for a couple of seconds and then disappear for two minutes. Concentrating on this point of light, I could distinguish the interior of a boat and the occupant's legs and hands. Since the light would only remain on for those few seconds, it was impossible to see exactly what type of activity was taking place.

After twenty minutes, I heard the familiar sound of a fish flopping on aluminum coming from the direction of the suspect boat. There appeared to be other boats on the water, but this particular craft was closest to our shoreline and therefore the easiest to discern through the binoculars. I continued to watch in the direction of the sound and two minutes later saw the same light. But this time, for just a second, I saw a pair of hands quietly putting a fish on a stringer! And then the light went off. A couple of minutes later the light again came on, and another fish was quickly placed on the thin rope. Given the care taken to avoid detection, I had to assume the fish were preseason walleyes.

Now, I had to contemplate my next move! Here were some fellows cheating before the season opener, taking advantage of all the legal fishermen while little could be done other than yelling at them to knock it off. But enforcement officers have a hard time thinking in this vein. We would much rather catch them in possession of the goods and issue a summons which would hopefully provide a deterrent to future illegal behavior. Also, folks who demonstrate this type of behavior are not likely to be first-time violators.

I studied the situation at hand: a boat sitting in total darkness with a stringer of illegal fish. I had no boat available to approach them. (A boat would do no good in this situation anyway as the fish would be discarded the minute I came close.) Any movement or lights on the shoreline would most likely spook them, allowing them to escape.

I pondered, What can I do? There's got to be a solution! How can I apprehend these guys under the existing conditions?

Then I made one of the most unconventional choices of my career. My options had been reduced to one: I would swim out to them!!

I removed my gun-belt and placed my billfold in one of my boots. Crawling slowly off the bank into the darkness, I quietly moved into the swampy, shallow water while maneuvering through the cattails and bulrushes that bordered the bay. It was incredibly cold, but I was so focused on my objective that the initial shock and numbness never became a concern. As the water rose to my waist, I stood motionless and tried to get a bearing on the boat. Finally, the glow of their light as they put another fish on the stringer was directly ahead of me about 60 feet away. If I could slide slowly and silently into the water, I would be able to swim to the boat without being discovered. My major concern at the moment was the possibility of getting tangled in their fishing lines if they happened to be fishing off my side of the boat.

It was now or never! I tried putting my C-cell flashlight in my mouth so I had both hands free, but I couldn't breathe. So I held it in one hand and eased out into the deeper water. As I swam the breast stroke to within ten feet of the boat, their light appeared, allowing me to distinguish the dimly lit face of the man in the stern and two other silhouettes. Now I knew I had three people with whom to contend.

My only thought was to get one quick peek at a walleye. That was all the evidence it would take to arrest the occupants for possession of fish during closed season. I was lucky so far; they were fishing on the opposite side of the boat and hadn't spotted me.

I swam up to the side of the boat trying desperately to see inside. Within seconds, their light came on again, so I had no choice but to grab the gunwales and lift myself up, over and into the interior of the 16-foot fishing boat. I hoped the shock value would give me enough time to determine if there was any evidence in plain view.

Over and in I went as I yelled, "CONSERVATION OFFI-CER—STAY WHERE YOU ARE!!" As if they could have gone anywhere! I found myself lying flat on my stomach in fish slime between the back and middle seats. I instantly rose to my knees and barked, "Stay calm. I just want to see your fish."

During the few seconds it took to get to this position, all hell broke loose in the boat; tackle boxes tipped over and got jumbled, accompanied by unintelligible hollering and screaming. As I directed my flashlight toward the operator, I saw the metal end of a rope stringer going into the water on the opposite side of the boat. I pointed the flashlight on the surface of the water and saw a cluster of white-tailed fish slowly sinking into the murky depths. I shouted, "What are you doing?" and instinctively plunged into the water after the stringer. All I thought was, THERE GOES MY EVIDENCE!! I'VE GOT TO GET THE FISH BACK! I dove down reaching for the rope and felt the end of the metal point. I made one more lunge and this time was able to get a solid hold of the cord.

As I surfaced with the stringer of fish in my right hand, I grabbed the side of the boat with my left while trying to catch my breath. I had the evidence, and a huge sense of satisfaction swept over me. Still hanging in the water grasping the side of the boat full of terrified fishermen, I realized my job wasn't over yet. Pulling myself up over the side and back into the boat while dragging the stringer of fish behind me, I asked if I could sit down and rest for a minute. In submissive voices, they said, "Sure. Sit down."

I tried to imagine what they were thinking during the past thirty seconds—sitting perfectly calm in a pleasant social surrounding, hauling in illegal fish like they've done for years, expecting no more than a limit of fish to take home, and WHAM, fishing as they know it comes to an abrupt end! I had probably resembled an oversize otter that slithered in and out of their boat looking for food!

My initial conversation with the three fish filchers involved reassurance that the Gestapo had not arrived but rather that I had been watching them catch illegal fish and this was the only method I could employ to catch them in the act.

All three eventually calmed down and even offered me a cup of coffee. I passed on their offer and described my intentions as to the enforcement action I would be taking. They still must have been in a state of disbelief because all they could say was, "Yes, that's fine. Whatever you have to do." Friendly chaps they were, cooperative, and admitting this was an affair that had been going on for years.

Nine walleyes were attached to the stringer. The method of operation was to begin fishing at dark, put the fish on a stringer in the water, and secure the stringer in place by stepping on it and holding it against the floor with foot pressure. Just raising a boot would allow for quick release in case they were ever checked or approached. That explained why all the fish were suddenly sinking when I unexpectedly arrived on the scene.

Disappointingly, the boat owner and chief author of this little operation was a local resort owner—rare for this kind of infraction. His two partners were clients from Illinois, and being nonresidents, it was now my duty to transport them to the county jail to post bail.

After driving to the sheriff's office and guiding them to the counter, the jailer asked why I was totally soaked. I told him a situation arose during these apprehensions that demanded some alternate protocols forcing me to take a dive. He glanced at me cynically and left it at that!

I drove home, changed into dry clothes, and proceeded to check legal fishermen after midnight. It was the start of another opening day!!

WOOF?

TEN

The Mistaken Identity

It was midafternoon two weeks before deer season when a call came in to the regional enforcement office, where I was picking up some paperwork. My supervisor handed me the phone and said it was about the sighting of an illegally taken deer, and it appeared to be in my patrol district. Two elderly gentlemen had been traveling north on a county dirt road 10 miles south of the office about fifteen minutes ago. They claimed they saw two young men dragging a deer out of the ditch and throwing it in the back of their toppered pickup. They also noticed the thrashing tail of the deer through the window as they drove around the truck. In addition, the truck had Colorado license plates, which is rare in this area.

I jumped in my patrol truck and headed south toward County Road 72. About ten minutes later, only 2 miles from the location of the initial description, I saw an approaching green pickup with a topper and noticed a green Colorado plate on the front bumper as it whizzed by. Immediately, I turned my vehicle around and engaged the red lights. It pulled over and two smiling young men exited. After approaching them and identifying myself, I told both that I had reason to believe that an illegal deer may have been transported in this truck and inquired if I could look in the back of their topper.

The young men's first reaction was laughter, followed by incredulous expressions. "Officer, you've got a true case of mistaken identity. We had an animal in the back all right, but it was a beaver. We've been trapping the flowages along 72 all week and just dragged one out of the ditch an hour ago."

I asked about the deer tail and the driver said, "Oh, that was our German shepherd. Yeah, I remember those two guys peering at us as they went by. I'll even take you home and show you the beaver and the trap!"

I told them I would still like to look in the back of their truck. They happily obliged and continued to laugh about what the witnesses obviously mistook for a deer. But just before closing the tailgate, I noticed a short hair about two inches long wedged between the inside fender panel and the floor. It was definitely a hollow deer-type hair, and I asked the two gentlemen about it. The driver said that he had just purchased the truck last month from his brother, an avid hunter in Colorado who had shot and transported many deer already this year.

I accepted their story and prepared to leave to answer several more calls before the end of the day. Nevertheless, my gut feeling told me to go one more step. I asked, "Since I'm going back your direction, could I just take a quick look in your garage? I'm sure there's nothing out of order, but I get paid to be curious, and this would let me put this call away and get on with my business."

"No problem," the driver said. "Just follow us."

I parked in front of the garage, walked toward the door, and just as I grabbed the handle, the owner said, "There's probably something in here you don't want to see."

And I was in fact quite startled when the first thing I saw lying on the floor in the entryway were two otters and a pile of traps. The otter season wouldn't be open for six weeks. I immediately walked through the next door to the car stall, and there in the dim light was a large, skinned buck deer hanging from the rafters.

"What's the story on this?" I said.

"Well, looks like you just hit the jackpot, officer. We shot this two days ago, and we were going to cut it up tonight."

"You mean this isn't the deer that was called in?"

"Nope! I told you those two guys didn't see what they said they saw."

After explaining the law and writing both individuals a summons for taking one deer and two otter during closed season, I began to ponder what had just happened: I had gotten a call from two men who completely misidentified an animal; I had stopped a truck that had transported a beaver, not a deer; I had encountered two young men who were so sure that I would dismiss any further searching that they took me to their residence; and then I had found a deer that had no connection to the information from the initial call. It was basically a random find of an illegal deer at a rural residence. So how much poaching really goes on before season?

A skinned buck deer found before season in a poacher's garage. Yet another random find.

ELEVEN

The Pike Pat-Down

Information received from the public in relation to game and fish violations is sporadic at best. The mind-set which prevents a person from going that extra step and reporting what he or she has witnessed or strongly suspected is nothing new in the chronicles of law enforcement. People plain and simple don't want to get involved after an illegal act has been observed or information has been acquired through friends or relatives. It takes a tremendous effort for a witness to move from discussing the event to actually picking up a phone and reporting a crime.

There are many reasons for this indifference. It ranges from common fear to distrust of the law enforcement community in maintaining anonymity to just being branded as a stool pigeon. This is especially true in game and fish enforcement.

Although most sportsmen's hearts are in the right place and they value justice, there seems to be a wall of comradeship that is difficult to break down. So when a call comes in that appears to expose an ongoing breach of the law, it's taken very seriously by all conservation officers and immediately becomes a top priority.

One such concerned citizen picked up a phone one hot Friday afternoon in July and relayed the fact that five fishermen in two vehicles were heading south out of state with a lot of fish. One was towing a U-haul trailer. He thought we might be interested in "checking them out." From the inflection in his voice, the anonymous caller seemed to be having a difficult time with his emotions and hung up quickly after declaring that the parties in question left fifteen minutes ago.

It was only about a twenty-minute drive for the vehicles to reach the city, and I was ten minutes out of town, so it would be a rush to intercept them, if it was even possible. I assumed they would be taking the most direct route of U.S. Highway 2, so as I kicked it down I called two other officers for assistance. Circumstances were in our favor that bright afternoon because the two officers and I were in position for only five minutes when we saw the two pickup trucks speeding south out of town.

The initial stop was no problem with both units pulling onto the shoulder and stopping in tandem. All five men jumped out and walked back to our patrol cars and asked us the reason for the delay. We explained to all five we had information they might be in possession of a large quantity of fish, possibly an over-limit, and these fish might be located in one of their vehicles.

I immediately observed their reactions for any signs of guilt or physical irregularities. They seemed cool and laid-back. Their talkativeness and casual demeanor remained steady during further questioning about the whereabouts of their fish. All of them agreed when questioned that the fishing was great in the area and that they had eaten all the fish they caught on their trip. They said they had no fish and that we could look through anything we wanted. I began having a slight doubt about the complaint call, but I'd seen this type of cool conduct before, and this wasn't going to dissuade us from searching, especially when consent had already been given.

Obviously the first place to look was the trailer being towed. I lifted the handle and opened the latch, allowing one of the doors to swing open. The thing was packed to the gills. There was every kind of fishing, camping and cooking gear imaginable. Sleeping bags and sacks of clothes rolled out onto the ground. Bundles of fishing rods, nets, tackle boxes and coolers were piled up to the roof. It was like a search nightmare knowing that everything would have to be removed in order to perform an adequate inspection. But this was a legitimate complaint so that's exactly what we started to do.

One by one, each article was taken from the trailer and laid on the ground. All this time, the gentlemen were continuing to claim they possessed no fish, especially after we had gone through five coolers full of food and kitchen items. After I had removed about two-thirds of the contents and had worked my way to the front of the trailer, which was finally visible, I heard a low hum or whine that sounded like a small, purring motor. Because of the road noise from the passing traffic, it was difficult to identify the exact location until I reached the far left corner of the trailer. Pulling back a mat, I put my hand on a white box. The container had a slight vibration in harmony with the sound. There it was in all its 6-cubic-foot glory: a 12-volt chest freezer. I signaled my fellow officers that I may have what we're looking for, and one of them brought a flashlight into the dark corner, opened the lid, and peered into the compartment.

"Yeah, looks like you're right. Appears to be many packages of something," he said.

My partner grabbed one of the packages, brought it out into the daylight, and asked the men what it was. There was no answer from any of the guys, so we opened it up, and we found ourselves holding five semi-frozen northern pike fillets. The white package marked "2 nort" on the outside, I assumed meant two northern pike. Either they counted wrong, or this was another deception tactic.

We removed all the packages from the freezer into a garbage bag and set them outside on the grassy ditch. Package after package, all containing an extra fillet, were lined up, opened and their contents counted. The fishermen, now turned suspects, were sitting in a cluster alongside the road hardly giving us a glance. They knew the little scheme was all over and were probably contemplating their punishment.

Some of the packages were frozen so hard that separating and counting without thawing was impossible. In those cases we just went by the package's markings. The total came to a minimum of 152 northern pike—137 over their limit! As we took the poachers to the courthouse a mile away, our conversations turned to the same topic they always do after we discover something like this: the greed factor and the accumulation mentality.

Approximately $3,900 in fines were assessed, but there's no guarantee that any monetary fine is a large enough deterrent to stifle this type of behavior. At the time of this violation, Minnesota statutes did not allow the court to revoke their fishing privileges, even though research has proven that removal of a person's right to hunt or fish is the most effective deterrent of them all. The new gross over-limit passed on March 1, 2003 allowing for license revocation would certainly have forced these guys to examine their behavior a little closer.

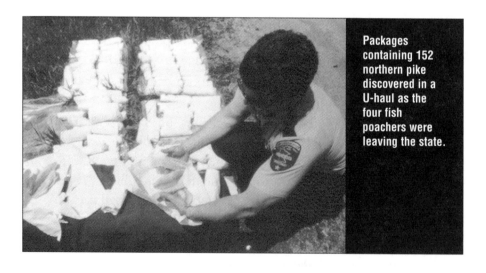

Packages containing 152 northern pike discovered in a U-haul as the four fish poachers were leaving the state.

TWELVE

The Chicago Two

A five-cabin resort situated in the midst of giant red and white pines overlooking a modest but exceptionally clear lake became an eagerly anticipated weekly stop on my enforcement rounds. The proprietors of this old-fashioned lodge provided the inspiration for my hundreds of visits over twenty-five years. We swapped stories, and both Hal and his wife possessed a great capacity for listening, in addition to spinning countless yarns. And I confess that the flavored coffee and home-baked cookies were an added inducement to take a swing down the narrow, mile-long driveway. Most of the initial chat centered around family, kids and the assortment of birds and animals spotted during the week. The latest jokes, world events, abnormal weather and local politics would usually consume the remainder of my coffee break.

However, some of the visits were totally devoted to "people behavior" and its long-term effect on a resort owner's sanity by Saturday morning checkout time. When it came to coping with customer quirks and wacky episodes, my two friends had accrued as many amazing encounters as I had over the years.

Hal's ten-year stint with the Natural Resource Department reinforced my favorite resort owner's lifetime commitment to environmental values, especially his desire to inform government officials and others as to the importance of protecting the visual quality of the forest. These traits more than qualified him to scrutinize some of the "goings on" among clients or friends of guests who stayed at their resort. It seems that the folks who would take advantage of them in their resort business, by stealing electricity for example, were often the same people who deceived the State by the act of poaching.

Most of my friends' customers were strong proponents of safeguarding the fish resource and respecting the rules of taking and possession. For many, catching one or two fish made their vacation investment worthwhile and satisfying. Some came to relax, read a book or simply enjoy the smells and remoteness of a northern Minnesota setting. To others, the numbers of fish caught, packaged and concealed were directly proportional to the quality of their trip—they were full-time stockpilers!

As midweek approached, Hal became curious about his father and son clients in Cabin 5. The pair seemed almost obsessed with fishing, leaving at first light and returning to the resort only after dark. The next hour would be spent in the fish cleaning house filleting and packaging fish for freezing. A hint of questionable activity arose when the owner emptied the pails of fish remains. Unless a tremendous amount of fish were being consumed, the numbers far exceeded any legal possession limits that he was aware of.

On Thursday evening Hal, the owner, decided it was time for a visit to the cleaning shack for no other reason than to talk about the fishing success on a couple neighboring lakes. "How's it going tonight, boys?" he asked as he pushed open the screen door.

"We did O.K. today . . . probably looks strange to see all these fish, but we have family licenses."

Hal immediately detected a tang of guilt sweeping over the two. "It doesn't work that way. If your wives, cousins, brothers-in-law or dogs are back in Chicago, you're limited to catching only your own fish. Your wives have to be actively involved. A 600-mile separation won't cut it!"

"Well . . . we've always done it this way," the son muttered with a less than sincere tone. "Besides, we've been coming here twenty years, and the license agent said it was O.K."

The duo was becoming increasingly defensive. This was their first stay at Hal's resort following nineteen years of vacationing at a nearby facility. They were grasping at straws with that remark, Hal sensed. All license sellers know better than that.

"I wish there was somebody who could explain all this to us," sputtered the cigar-chomping father, his two-inch stogie in sync with every movement of his devious lips.

"I've got just the person who could enlighten you on the whole thing," Hal answered with an accommodating air. "I'll see if he'll stop up tomorrow."

When I arrived, the older gentleman was down by the lake cleaning out his minnow bucket in the chilly water. "Hi there... name's Tom. I was told you had some questions about fish regulations. Maybe I could help if you had a little time to spare."

The pungent smoke from his thick cigar circled above as he turned and rose from his crouched position. His puffing tempo rapidly increased after he spotted the uniform and in a deep, but anxious voice, he growled, "Yeah . . . yeah . . . my boy's cleaning fish . . . let's go up there."

The kid was trembling so bad, I thought he would slice a finger off while he was separating the skin from a bass fillet. After introductions, it became plain as the nose on his ashen face that something fraudulent was in the works—I needed to look in their freezer!

"What-da-ya say, boys. How 'bout going back to your cabin and discussing the regs over a cup of coffee. Maybe I could take a quick look at your fish, too, if that would be O.K. with you."

While all three of us squeezed around the small table sipping on hastily brewed decaf, I silently mulled over my options. I could continue explaining the laws (that they already knew) or I could ask permission to take a peek in the top freezer compartment of the refrigerator. Sucking on his second nauseating cigar, the father seemed to be getting more comfortable with my presence—so this was the critical moment: "Can I take a quick peak in your freezer before I leave?"

"Yeah, go ahead. Most of them are rock bass."

Right away I regarded his statement as peculiar. Most fishermen don't keep rock bass which is considered by many to be unpalatable—a species with no limit. I pulled open the top freezer compartment and two packages slipped out onto the linoleum floor. Fixing my eyes on the remainder of the wrapped bundles, I noted the black print on each: 2 perch-4 rock bass-1 crappie. And another: 5 rock bass-1 northern-one bass.

"I'm gonna unwrap a couple of these just to verify their contents, sir," I said in a more official voice. "Might have to use the sink over here to thaw them out."

It took only a few minutes to determine what I had already assumed; all 48 brown freezer-wrapped packages were falsely marked. None of them contained what was so neatly described on the outside . . . these guys were well aware of the law!!

"You fellas have some explaining to do. Wanna talk about it?" A subdued atmosphere permeated the room as I removed the entire collection.

"No, I guess we didn't understand the law . . . I mean . . . well . . . I know we're in trouble," they stuttered.

After a full count, a hefty over-limit of largemouth bass and 150 crappies were identified—120 over the limit! Multiplying this by twenty years adds up to stealing a big chunk of resource.

These two fish poachers embodied the poorest of sportsmen's mind-sets: greed! This was further demonstrated when both of them stated to Hal, "He took all our fish . . . what's the use of staying here any longer?" They were totally clueless about any other purpose for a vacation in Minnesota. Finally, as the father was writing out the rental check, he looked up at Hal and asked, "What's your name?" There was no doubt that he would have signed the owner's name to the bottom of the check, thus making it worthless with payment most likely irretrievable, if Hal hadn't picked up on the subtle inquiry.

In the following week, Hal had an opportunity to speak to the person from whom he had purchased the freezer in the poachers' cabin. "Warren, do you know how many fish the freezer holds in that refrigerator you sold me last year? . . . FIFTEEN HUNDRED DOLLARS WORTH!"

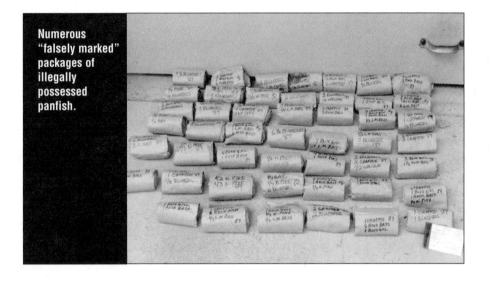

Numerous "falsely marked" packages of illegally possessed panfish.

THIRTEEN
The Dead Decoy

U ndercover work during waterfowl season was seldom boring. An officer's job consisted of monitoring hunters' behavior by picking a good vantage point without giving away his identity. Many times scattered hunting groups could be observed simultaneously for various infractions, such as unplugged guns, shooting before or after hours, taking a protected species or over-limit. Observing violations was infrequent and sporadic; most duck hunters made an effort to follow the rules.

Nevertheless, although uncommon, some folks would try to skirt the laws and occasionally take advantage of a situation.

It appeared this would be another average daybreak in the marsh for my partner and me. We had chosen this particular little lake that crisp morning only because neither of us had been on it before—it was new territory to work. The sun had risen enough to help distinguish two hunting parties a quarter mile apart, blended in among the tall sedge-grasses. It turned out they were all set up—decoys bobbing out in front of their heavily camouflaged blinds and boats hidden among the cattails. We determined that situating ourselves between the groups would provide the most advantageous lookout.

The first peak of the orange sun above the horizon reflected off the heads of the four decoys we had set out before fading back into the bulrushes. Instead of shotguns, we cradled broom handles in our arms to look like duck hunters from a distance.

It didn't take long for the shooting to start. Both locations were producing a great deal of action, although very few ducks were hit. The ducks appeared confused, flying in all directions and even landing in our measly decoy set.

After the local ducks finally settled down or left the lake, there was a pause in the shooting accompanied by a gentle breeze that forced the decoys to rock and swing in different directions. In fact the breeze caused one of our plastic replicas to free itself from its anchor—it begin drifting down the lake toward the west hunting party. As it continued toward the middle of the pond, our decoy was pushed away from the blinds by the increasing wind until it settled in the lily pads about 100 feet from the opposite shoreline.

That's when we heard the noise of an outboard motor cord being pulled. PLA-pla-pla . . . PLA-pla-pla . . . PLA-pla-pla-ROOOM!–Someone in the blind to our west finally got their little engine started.

Seconds later, a small boat with two camouflaged men emerged from the rushes. Peering through my binoculars, it was easy to make out the bowman clutching a gun barrel flashing in the sun. At full bore, the boat raced across the waves directly toward our marooned decoy. About 100 yards away and drifting to their target, we could hear the outboard settle down to an idle. "They're going to pick up our decoy for us," I said to my partner. "But what's with the gun?"

It wasn't five seconds when, BOOM . . . BOOM! The guy in the front of the boat was blasting at our decoy! Was it even possible that our fake bird looked authentic enough to mistake it for the real thing? It seemed doubtful until, BOOM, the final shot. It just wouldn't die! So what kind of characters are we going to have to deal with here, I thought.

We both now agreed that these "hunters" should be checked out as soon as possible before the pellets start flying in our direction. They were already heading back to their blind when we pulled up alongside. "How's the duck hunting this morning?" I shouted over the hum of the engines.

"We've done O.K."

"We're a couple of game wardens. Just wondering about that uncased gun there. I'd like to take a look at it." Of course, the shotgun was empty by now. Then the inevitable question. "Do you have a book on duck identification, and if so, what kind of duck did you just shoot at?" (I thought a little humbling experience never hurt anybody.)

"Is that your decoy?" the operator said.

I replied it was one of ours that "got away." That's when the bowman came unglued.

"You mean you put that out there so we would shoot at it? That's a poor #*(%*@* way to write tickets on unsuspecting legal hunters like us. This whole thing is a case of entrapment!"

Instead of choosing a calm demeanor, this guy was taking the offensive. He continued his tirade while we were checking licenses and explaining their wrongdoings. When this brought him little satisfaction, he started in with the threats: "Wait till I get back home. I know lots of people. You guys will pay for this . . . " And on and on it went.

After explaining that no set-up was intended and that taking ducks from a motorboat was illegal, we all proceeded to his cabin to retrieve a license he had mistakenly left there. Pulling up to the dock, I noticed a rod and reel with a line and baited hook leading into the water.

"Does this belong to you, sir?"

"Yeah, it's mine! I suppose that's illegal, too."

"Actually it is," I shot back. "A set line has always been illegal in Minnesota."

I could tell he was seething at our presence, so our best option was to issue a summons and leave as soon as possible. It wasn't until I looked at his hunting license that I recognized the name. "You wouldn't happen to be the former Chief of Information and Education for the State DNR?" I inquired.

"I am!" he snapped. "And now I own a big newspaper. You'll be seeing this whole outrageous scheme of yours in print next week, I guarantee you!"

Well, he was right on that! It sure helps when you're the editor of a newspaper and you can slant the editorial for your own purposes. While reading his lengthy opinion, I was not certain it referred to the same incident. And I was there! The public got a very skewed version of a "run-in" with a couple of nasty, malicious and spiteful game wardens in northern Minnesota who used underhanded tactics to do their job. I had hoped after he sat back and examined his behavior that he would take some responsibility and come to a different conclusion. So be it!

It's still satisfying to know that these types of encounters are rare and that this individual's attitude represents a tiny minority of the hunting public.

Outdoors with
Carlson Markhart

What does it profit a man if he gain a mallard yet loses 50 clams to the friendly conservation officer? A pretty guilty conscious, judging from the story a friend of ours had to tell this past week.

It seems he and another guy were hunting ducks on opening day up north some place. They knocked down a mallard but the bugger went under on them and they spent the next hour or so looking in the heavy reeds.

Finally, one of them spotted what looked like a downed bird clear across the small bay in which they were hunting. Unthinking, the pair started the motor and headed across the water, getting just close enough to finish off the bird before he disappeared again.

The driver cut the motor and the front man cut loss -- at a decoy. Right behind the pair came this little motorized canoe with two men in it.

"State conservation officers", they said. "May we see your licenses?"

To make a long story short, the two were each tagged for carrying loaded guns in a motorized vehicle.

Oh, yes, the decoy belonged to the two wardens. They had scattered several of them around the lake.

"What I want to know, Carlson, is should we have gone to court on that thing since the wardens were baiting people with those decoys?" the friend asked.

Well, a guy might make a case out of the thing. Conservation officers have been known to purposely bait suspected outlaws with such things as mounted deer heads nailed to trees and ducks with flight feathers pinioned. And courts have been known to give them heck for it.

But fighting the thing would probably end up costing the guy more than the $50 bail money he lost and, after all, he did violate the law by not unloading and casing his gun before chasing his "cripple".

He thought, he said, that he was doing the right thing by trying to retrieve a downed duck. "Would we have gotten a tag if we hadn't gone after the bird?" he asked.

That is a good possibility, we admitted, since our friend acknowledged that the two conservation officers had been watching them for some time and saw the duck go down, and since it is illegal not to try to retrieve downed birds.

The two men in question are normally pretty good sportsmen and don't violate game laws just for the heck of it. In our minds, they simply forgot themselves for the moment and did a dumb thing.

You can't fault the conservation officers for doing their job. They saw a violation and they acted -- never mind that they were partially the cause for the violation, that there was a vaguely legitimate reason for it and that they would have been better off out in the woods investigating the cause of all the deer rifle shots that morning.

This editorial published by the violator in the newspaper he owned, presents his skewed version of the decoy-blasting incident.

FOURTEEN

The Canned Message

Not very often is a dog able to chase and take down a healthy whitetail deer. Harass them, yes, but to actually catch a deer and do harm occurs only during a harsh winter when eight weeks or more of bitter cold and deep snow have reduced a deer's natural defenses to a point of severe distress or starvation. Such harsh winters occur once or twice every ten years, but when they do, a pack of local dogs, or even a loner, can do extreme damage to a yarded herd of deer, or occasionally even obliterate the entire population.

Killing a family pooch is not a duty that any warden relishes. Few counties have a "leash law" prohibiting dogs from running free. However, Minnesota law requires us to take action when complaints of killing or chasing arise. The same law also puts the burden on the owner, who is liable and is subject to a fine for allowing a dog to run free. The first order of business is to make an attempt to find the owners, but when that fails, more drastic measures have to be taken to protect our resource.

An especially deep snow during a mid-seventies winter preceded a spring of incredibly punishing conditions for our local deer. Cedar feeding areas and heavy coniferous swamps south of Grand Rapids were crisscrossed with 3-foot ruts carved by large groups of struggling animals pushing snow up to their chests. In mid-March, a crust formed on the melting snow's surface overnight, preventing already exhausted deer from getting to food sources only 30 feet from the trail. Deer were slowly starving until the spring temperatures rose enough to melt the snow completely.

Many rural dogs located these weakened populations, and their primitive instincts prevailed. The size and breed of dog had no bearing on the dog's desire to kill; they were pets transformed into wolves. The morning was the critical time for their killing sprees. The snow, still crusty after a cold night, would support the dogs' weight and allow them to take long romps far from home over the frozen surfaces. A pack of mutts would actually form a hierarchy, the largest and strongest dog assuming leadership. Totally at the mercy of the frozen environment, the deer had little chance of escaping the killing frenzy of a dog pack.

Just after sunrise, I patrolled the edges of yards known to have "pack dogs," looking intently for fresh canine tracks entering the woods. Following a light snow was most productive when I could tell if the dogs were presently in the area.

The first set of tracks was quite large, ambling ahead of two smaller imprints. The thin crust was unable to hold my weight, forcing me to limit my forward stumbling to the deer trails. I kept my eyes on the fresh paw marks that progressed deeper into the forest. Within five minutes of my grueling march, I spotted the first sign of mutilation: a yearling deer lay half buried 3 feet off the deep path. It appeared to have hardly struggled while raging teeth had torn it apart. Dogs on a deer mission seldom eat their prey; they only kill for the primal thrill!

Twenty yards farther was another red swirl of devastation. Two more fawns lay a few feet apart amid a layer of brown and white hair strewn about the otherwise white surface. Dog tracks, old and new, trailed from this site and continued along the rutted path.

Before my morning trek was finished, I witnessed 16 carcasses of deer, all slaughtered and left for the ravens and coyotes to complete the feeding cycle. The suspects in this mass murder were probably at home by now, sleeping off their all-night excursion on the front porch, their masters oblivious to "Fido's" whereabouts the last six hours.

I concluded that it was going to take additional manpower to track down these dogs before more carnage occurred.

Two neighboring officers arrived at dawn the next morning to help. Armed with rifles, we each followed different paths into the heavy cedars, hoping to spot the slayers. Fresh tracks again led us along the furrows and to additional remains of dead deer. Six more fresh kills, including two does, were scattered under the low-hanging branches, every one displaying the telltale signs of canine annihilation. The total deer lost were at 22 so far, and these only included those we happened to hit upon; the real figure was most likely double. Unless our luck improved, odds were the entire herd would soon be destroyed.

A stack of 22 deer carcasses found after a four-day killing spree by one dog.

The third morning offered a more hopeful resolution. I asked Bill, a wildlife biologist friend, to scan the area for dog activity from the air. Bill said that he and his pilot would take a look on their way to a coyote telemetry project south of the yard. The first pass of the Cessna 172 signaled no indication of concern, but the next circling swung directly over us at tree-top level. I could see hand gestures from the plane's cockpit while it swooped overhead again, but any signal Bill was trying to send to us was unintelligible. Our major predicament became all too clear; we had no radio communication.

I signaled to him from the ground to make one more fly-by; maybe this time I could decipher his arm-flailing signs. Nope! With only two seconds to work with and the sun reflecting off the cockpit's windows, reading Bill's hand signals was nearly impossible.

"Here he comes again," I yelled at my partner. "All I can see is the belly of the plane." Just as the wing's shadows swept over our position, the passenger door opened and a small object was dropped in our direction. I ran to the shiny item and snatched it from the snow bank. Written on the outside of an empty oil can was a hastily scratched note: "DOG IN FIELD TO SOUTH—HAS DEER DOWN NOW." So much for modern radio systems when you've got an oil can handy!

A point of trees lay just to our south jutting into a snow-covered hay field. I guessed the critter was around the corner less than 200 yards away. As we crawled to the last edge of concealment, I peeked around the brush and over the drifts. There he was, a husky-style dog matching the complaints I'd received over the last two weeks. It appeared to have just pulled a deer down and was in the final stages of dispatching the large doe.

"Easy now . . . e-a-s-y," I said to myself as I slowly squeezed the trigger of my scoped rifle. One loud crack ended our three-day hunt.

The 60-pound killer was in fact the dog that had been brutalizing the township's deer herds for the past two weeks, including the doe in the field that was carrying two fetuses.

I retrieved over 30 carcasses from this single deer-wintering site but had no idea how many more were actually killed by this one dog. Two smaller mongrel-types were also seen roaming the vicinity, but the next two weeks revealed no more fresh deer kills. Other nearby areas investigated during that early spring brought the total to over 100 dog-killed deer.

When wardens catch up with deer-killing canines, the dogs pay the price. However, the real fault lies not with the dogs but with their masters, whose negligence leads to the very preventable loss of hundreds of Minnesota deer. Too many pet owners are still oblivious to the devastation that free-running dogs inflict on deer during harsh winters. Only continued educational efforts by the DNR and increased cooperation by dog owners will end the slaughter in the snow.

A 66-pound Malamute dog shot by officer next to the 23rd and 24th deer killed. The doe on the left contained two unborn fawns.

FIFTEEN

The Dripping Cedars

The spring of the year is a season Minnesota game wardens hunger for. The increased warmth from the sun embraces the plants and critters awakening from their long cold snooze. The doldrums of a long winter diminish in April as the local creeks begin accepting the run-off from the melting snows; it's just a matter of days until the first cycle of northern pike appears in the streams. The spawning period has arrived.

To a few, it's time for unraveling their gill nets and deciding on a special place to reap some preseason fish. To the local game warden, it's time to modify his work routine and prepare for long hours of night surveillance. The pursuit of fish poachers has begun!

The afternoon was sunny and especially warm for mid-April. Bouncing along on some back roads, I decided to check a pair of creeks for flow and water temperature. Surprisingly, a narrow brook dumping into the Swan River was already reading 40 degrees—a perfect temperature for northern pike to embark on their two-week spawning mission.

It was time for a closer look downstream. Immediately upon entering some thick brush emerging from semifrozen swamp, I spied a florescent orange ribbon, encapsulated by many years of growth, attached from a cedar tree. The rings of woody fiber had almost concealed its color if it were not for another, fresher ribbon circling the trunk just above it.

Hiking farther into the dark, icy slough, I discovered another orange speck jutting from an overhanging cedar tree. The conditions were the same as before except that the fresher ribbon was wrapped around the tree growing beside it. As I studied the jumble of cedars ahead, I could make out a crude line of ribbons leading through the tangle of trees, brush and frozen clumps. The conditions became so thick that it was incredible to think anyone would have ventured this far. But there they were—ribbons, old and new, snaking a path through the jungle.

Another sluggish and tortuous half-mile slog brought me to a small grassy meadow along the bank of the creek where the little orange markers finally ended. The little hump of dry grass and sand confirmed signs of human activity—footprints, newly cut saplings and an empty can emitting a fresh beer odor. Somebody had been here. And recently!

I explored the sand mound only to find more tracking in and out of the water, plus two 8-foot cut popple poles. My survey led me to the heavy cedar trees that bordered the little island of gravel, where footpaths disappeared under their low-hanging, aromatic branches. After I found a spot to stand up, I felt a water droplet land on my head, and then another . . . and another. It hadn't rained for days and the cozy warmth of the sun could be felt through the tops of the trees. I knew something was amiss as I gazed directly overhead. There, straight above me, were two dripping gill nets strung up among the thick cedar limbs. The two links of mesh were a foot apart, fastened about ten feet up in the boughs.

It's time to leave!! Get out now before you're spotted—if you haven't been already—and get help for this evening, I thought to myself. I struggled back to my truck by an alternate route.

Immediately I informed my neighboring officers of my discoveries. Within two hours I was meeting with three wardens to plan our strategy. We decided to put the first section of the ribboned path under surveillance and just wait for activity—all night if necessary!

It didn't take long at all. Just at dusk, two men wearing hipboots and toting backpacks walked down the driveway of a residence opposite the trail, crossed the road and disappeared into the shadowy swamp.

Now we had to witness them in the act. This wouldn't be easy considering the noisy march ahead that would force us to tread lightly through the ice and muck of a twisted, sloppy terrain . . . in the dark!! Two officers remained back at the road and two of us headed into the darkness. Quietly we moved and stumbled over the thick shards of broken ice until we arrived within hearing distance of our targets. "There they are," I whispered. "See their lights?"

A slight glow could be seen through the branches 50 feet from their position. There were no voices, just the sounds of rustling feet and poles being dropped in the water. A closer scan with the binoculars illuminated the whole scene. Both men were maneuvering poles between the creek's surface and the sandy beach. Attached to each shaft was a 6-foot gill net. One would be placed in the shallow water for two minutes, lifted out and placed on the sand. The second person would remove the fish from the net while the first person would place the other pole and net in the depths.

Within twenty minutes and ten dips of the nets, the two fish poachers were packing up. This was the slickest method I'd ever seen to take fish in such a short period—these guys were bona fide poaching veterans!

Hiding behind a 6-foot-high vertical root system from a fallen cedar tree, I hunched and waited for the duo to walk by. Crunch, crunch, crunch, they approached. "Game wardens! Stop where you are!" We yelled as my partner and I drenched them with floodlights.

These were some stunned boys! And they weren't exactly boys—they were older gentlemen carrying heavy, bulging packs on their backs. As they stood shaking and speechless, we removed the sacks and let the fish thieves sit down to catch their breath. After their gasps and panting subsided, we called in the other two officers to assist with the apprehension and interviewing. They said little other than we certainly were an unexpected part of their conspiracy.

Dumping out the packs' contents, we counted over 25 shiny northern pike—later weighing a total of 85 pounds. How many nights they had been netting was only a guess, and by leaving the nets in the trees again, this obviously wasn't going to be the last time.

Two well-known members of the local community were finally caught supplying the fire department with fish for their in-house feeds. They both hinted that guilty pleas would be submitted in court the following morning.

However, the older gentleman had a change of heart that crucial next day. I was watching out the window, awaiting the twosome's arrival, when they approached the steps of the court. The younger man turned to the older for a second, turned back toward the door, and walked into the building beneath us. The older man stood for a minute, looked up at the structure, then turned and walked away. Nobody saw him again for three years!!

He ultimately paid a penalty (fine and short jail spell) when an outstanding warrant returned him to his home ground.

Two short gill nets and 86 pounds of northern pike seized from two fish poachers after dark.

SIXTEEN
The Three Amigos

S itting out all hours of the night waiting for deer shiners to materialize could get darn boring if action was minimal. And that was a large part of the time. We tried our best to choose fields or backroads that either "looked good" or had generated the most complaints about shooting and shining. But even armed with premium information and years of instinct, it was still a crap-shoot, a game that by-and-large put us at the mercy of the jack-lighters' impulses.

Sprawled out atop the warm hood of my patrol vehicle, I was getting too comfortable under the heavy sleeping bag. Nodding off was my chief obstacle. The silence was interrupted only by periodic radio chatter that couldn't drown out my partner's constant inquiries about my current alertness. As a non-coffee drinker, my chances of staying awake were minimal compared with his eight cups of jittery determination.

Our work party this quiet, starry evening, consisted of three vehicles, each situated 5 miles apart. Nothing of significance had been seen or heard for over an hour other than the occasional muted hum of our surveillance plane drifting 6,000 feet above. It was two nights before the opening day of deer season, so anticipation ran high among the officers compared to the previous fall evenings.

My co-worker to the west had just finished dining earlier that evening with four of his area acquaintances, one of them now his civilian riding partner. The other three had inquired about his plans and where he may be working tonight. Willy told them he was going to plant himself on a field north of town for the rest of the night. . . . He went south!

Just past 11:00 P.M., the crack of Willy's voice over the speaker jolted me from the comfy hood as I scrambled to a position behind the steering wheel. "They just shot one right on the field next to us!" he shouted. "We're going to get behind them."

The pilot radioed, "I'll head over your direction . . . couple minutes away."

We were parked only a few feet from Highway 6 when the next transmissions gave the direction the suspect car was moving, "We're going toward 6." A few minutes later, Willy bellowed, "Now they're heading south on 6 . . . we're right on their tail."

The car was speeding toward us! Our plan was to block its path by parking halfway across the roadway. We assumed they would slow to a stop once they approached our flashing red lights.

The plane was already overhead when the pilot sighted the two southbound streaking vehicles. Now only two miles north of our position, Willy radioed concern that his engine was overheating and he was losing ground on the culprits. Finally Willy hollered, " I think my engine blew! I'm dead in the water. They should be just about on ya, Tom." Glancing north, I could see a faint light reflecting in the sky; the glow increased until I spotted two headlights bouncing in our direction.

"That's the one, Tom," shouted the pilot. "Stop it there!"

I thought it unwise to remain inside, so both of us scurried for the ditch while the pulsing red lights illuminated the road and trees. "Here it comes . . . watch out, it's not slowing down!" We stared in amazement as the sleek-looking sedan roared past the lit-up blockade, barely missing our front bumper. "Time to go," I hollered, jumping back in the car and beginning the southbound pursuit.

Jerry's voice from the cockpit was now controlling the show. "You're going to have to kick it down," he declared. "These guys are movin'. They're already two miles ahead of you, Tom."

"I'll do what I can, Jerry. But we're topped out at 96 now. Doubt if we can overtake before Remer."

"That might be a problem." Jerry shot back. "Now that it's on a straight stretch, I'm losing ground myself! I'm flat out at 135 in the Cub and I can't stay with them. If they get to town before me, I'll lose visual contact if they turn their lights off. They must be doing close to 150 miles per hour."

The urgency of the situation raised my fears that even with our eye in the sky, the chances of apprehension were diminishing every second. The pilot continued to report the car's distance from town until he shouted, "Brake lights . . . it's turning around . . . hold on . . . it's cross-ways in the road. Tom, you're only a mile or so behind . . . better start slowing down."

It didn't take long at 95 mph to make out the lights of their stopped car after popping over the next hill. Screeching to a semi-controlled stop next to the front door, we aimed our flashlights at the three wide-eyed violators who were standing outside. All three men were compliant and sheepish as we positioned them in front of the headlights and applied handcuffs. None appeared very upset about getting caught or being temporarily restrained.

"What's the problem with your car?" I asked.

"It overheated when we tried to turn around. You never would have caught us if we could have kept going!"

"That may be," I retorted. "But it's water over the dam now . . . isn't it?!"

At this point, four other officers had arrived to assist in the processing of the three fleeing bandits. A wrecker was summoned to transport the seized 1970 Pontiac TransAm to the impound lot in Grand Rapids. Willy said he thought the deer he had witnessed being shot was a large buck and that he would retrieve it for evidence on the way home.

More surprises surfaced as the roadside processing continued. Willy's civilian rider turned out to be the brother of one of the shiners. Plus the whole crew were Willy's earlier dinner guests! "You can't even tell the truth to your friends when you're in this business," Willy snarled as he secured the last set of restraints.

Although this case comprised an unusual set of circumstances, the betrayal of friendship wasn't all that unexpected. As a law enforcement officer, you constantly struggle with the feeling not to put every person you meet into the same kettle of suspects who might violate a game law. We all recognize that it's a small minority of folks that show complete disregard for the resource rules, but sometimes an officer's positive perception of human nature, particularly the trust factor, tends to diminish a bit following an incident like this. Like Willy said later that evening, "You just never know."

This is the speedy '69 Pontiac TransAm that led officers on an 150-mile-per-hour chase.

SEVENTEEN

The Empty Freezer

Many of the fishing violations discovered originate from folks developing what we call an "accumulative mentality." This seems to start out with a few successful days in a row of possessing more fish than they can eat or immediately give away.

In time, with additional productive fishing outings, they begin to accrue so many fish that a personal "giveaway program" gets going. This could be friends giving away fish to friends, fellow employees, relatives or even to social events such as church fish fries. Sometimes it is carried to the point of actually selling the fish for a profit. This is the chief reason for the possession law that allows only one limit of fish per person at any time, no matter where it may be stored. If it is respected, this law is a definite resource protector by establishing a more even playing field among the fisherpersons who must share a limited fish population.

These "accumulative mentality" people can be locals who have an expert knowledge of fish-biting times and locations, or they can be nonresidents who visit for extended periods of time, sometimes through the entire summer. Most sportsmen respect the possession limits and know why it is so necessary to abide by them, but the few that don't can wreak havoc on the resource and sometimes even cause enough damage to ruin a fish population for years.

One particular case back in the early 1980s illustrates this frame of mind. For seven years I'd known something illegal was going on with a couple from Indiana. This husband and wife team in their early sixties owned a cabin near a small lake 20 miles north of Grand Rapids. The first year I had just a hint that these folks were stocking up on fish—mainly crappies—but the following years yielded further information that there were indeed a lot of fish being stockpiled in their cabin and that their little scheme had been going on for the last twelve seasons.

The crappie may be "only a panfish," but you have to live in northern Minnesota to comprehend the importance most fishermen attach to this little fish. "Where are the crappies biting?" is the most frequently asked question of all conservation officers wherever this fish exists in any numbers. If you know of a fertile crappie hole, it could be one of the biggest secrets you carry to your grave! (Even friends respect your reluctance to disclose these locations.) Besides, it's one of the few tasty fish whose season is open all year long.

The problem with catching these crappie poachers was the lack of details available on the day, time or even month that they journeyed back to Indiana. With such sketchy information, there was no way to obtain a search warrant, and getting consent to search wasn't even an option. Hearsay information is better than nothing, because at least it gets you focused on a potential problem, but it does little to get you in the door. So it becomes a waiting and watching game.

In the course of my patrolling this vicinity during the fall of the years, I would try to notice some little factor that might tip me off to a possible departure. I also got the word out to a couple confidants in the area who passed by the cabin on a regular basis and asked them to call me if they saw the people leaving.

Finally, after seven years and many futile hours of surveillance, a call came to my home late one autumn night from one of my friendly informants. He wondered if I'd be interested in knowing that this was the first time that he had seen the suspect's van backed into his cabin instead of being pulled straight in. There was zero hesitation on my part. If I had been sleepy when I picked up the phone, I wasn't after that statement. "I'm on my way, talk to you later," I said!

Diving for my uniform in the dark and scampering out the door into the crisp night air, I pointed my patrol vehicle north and reeled off the 27 miles in less than a half an hour. After hiding my vehicle a quarter mile away, I crawled through the brush directly across the road from the blue van. Next to the van was an older model, full-size Chrysler sedan, which was also backed toward the cabin.

It was now after 1:00 A.M., and there were lights on in the house and movement back and forth from the rear of both vehicles. They were leaving soon. Less than ten minutes passed when suddenly all the lights went off and both vehicles were started. I was surprised to see two vehicles ready to go since it was never the norm to have more than one car heading south in a situation like this. I was still sure that there were only two people involved. I didn't dare approach them at this point in time because it is difficult to take control without assistance in a situation like this, especially when you are unsure exactly where the fish may be located. Also, it is easier to legally search a vehicle without a warrant if enough evidence suggests that a violation may have occurred. Once I saw movement inside the van's cab, I scurried back to my unit, only to look back down the road and see both vehicles heading south. Radioing ahead for assistance to a fellow officer located south of me, I continued following them far behind to avoid suspicion. Upon entering the north side of Grand Rapids, I decided it was time to make an attempt to stop them. There was enough reasonable suspicion to check these folks out due to the time of night and the accumulation of complaints over the years.

The van and the sedan were about 300 feet apart when I hit the red lights. Almost instantly the brake lights lit up on the blue van that I was directly behind, but the sedan kept going and even seemed to speed up. (Later we found out that they were communicating by C.B. radio.) It was a good thing I had help as my fellow officer stopped the sedan at an intersection 6 blocks ahead. It appeared to us that the driver was trying to make a getaway.

We directed both into a nearby mall parking lot where the two occupants were ordered out of the vehicles. Mr. Driver in the van was very cooperative after I explained the reasons and suspicions for the stop. However, this attitude was not shared by Mrs. Driver, who was visibly and vocally upset at our presence, which was a good sign that something might be out of place. But it wasn't long until disappointment replaced our suspicions when Mr. Driver said, "Go ahead and look in the freezer. There's nothing in it anyway. I couldn't fish much this year because of my broken leg."

In the rush of the stop, I never noticed that he was on crutches and was having a tough time getting around. I opened the tailgate and there in the back was a 16-cubic-foot freezer taking up most of the whole space. Disappointment gave way to total frustration; as I peeked in the freezer with my flashlight, it was totally empty!! Nothing!

Asked if there were any fish on board either of the two vehicles, the couple's answer was an emphatic, "No!" Mrs. Driver was getting more irate and her "I told you so's" were starting to saturate the damp night air. I couldn't believe it. Seven years and I pick the one where he was physically unable to fish. And another thing, according to the information from my witnesses, that freezer usually was carrying 5,000 to 6,000 crappies! (That was what they were reportedly taking back every year for the last twelve years.) Well, I said to myself, let's take one last shot and look in the sedan, even with all of Mrs. Driver's huffiness. She just about came unglued when I said I would like her to open the trunk.

"Why do you keep pushing the issue? We told you we have no fish. We're going to sue." She stood there motionless as everything was removed from the trunk area, including boxes of clothing, pillows and other items. I then reached behind the spare tire and felt some cardboard boxes. After a great deal of pulling and squeezing, three boxes were loosed from their confines and placed on the blacktop for further inspection.

Our expectations really weren't any higher until I saw the first container of fillets, a frozen milk carton filled to the brim. And then another one and another until all the boxes were opened revealing at least 20 cartons and containers of fish fillets. There weren't 6,000 fish, but there were enough to constitute a major violation of the limit rules. After counting and estimating the amount of mostly frozen fish, including some admissions from Mr. Driver, the total registered at over 600 fish–1,200 fillets!

Obviously, the intent to violate the law was overwhelming. My "informants" appeared to be right on. If indeed it hadn't been for the broken leg, the 6,000 crappies in transit wouldn't have been out of the question. In a way I was glad the outcome was lower than expected–less resource been abused. The plan was to remove the fish from the unassuming sedan and transfer them to the van's freezer once out of state. Five to six thousand crappies over 12 years, add it up–lots of resource going south!

As for the two fish poachers, a substantial bail was posted that morning, and they were released to continue their trip home. At the time, even for such a large violation, both violators' fishing rights could not legally be revoked. In other words, they could continue to fish the next day! Most of the fish were taken out of just one lake. It took many years for the crappie population in that lake to replenish itself, and I don't imagine it is still as abundant as it used to be. I truly believe the most dangerous piece of equipment used to take fish is the basic hook and line in the hands of those who intend to violate the possession laws.

An estimated 600 crappies taken from the wife's car as she and her husband were leaving the state at 2:00 A.M.

EIGHTEEN

The Elusive Bug Deflector

Many calls about deer poaching are from the concerned public who witness events very close to their homes. This makes sense because rural residents are tuned to the day-to-day normal behavior in the area, and anything that seems out of place or just not right draws attention. Conservation officers try to build up good relationships and rely on these folks, many who are hunters themselves, to provide the detection and reporting of illegal behavior in their neighborhoods.

A good example of this is a call I received one sunny afternoon during the second day of a sixteen-day deer season. A landowner living along a blacktopped county road heard two shots directly in front of her home. Looking out of the picture window, she saw a pickup truck stopped in the middle of the road and a young person outside standing next to the cab. She saw the driver then get back in the cab and drive off to the north. Curious if an animal was shot, the witness walked across the road and noticed a shot deer lying about 20 yards into the woods. She immediately called me to investigate, as it seemed strange that the deer would not have been retrieved. I asked her if she could describe the older brown Ford pickup any further.

"Well, would this be important?" she said. "I noticed a bug deflector on the front that read 'DEER HUNTER.'"

Immediately, I recognized that particular vehicle as one that I'd seen many times in the area and in town over the last couple of years. I thanked her for the call and said I would contact her after I found the culprit. This particular violation was consistent with many law abuses during a Minnesota deer season: illegally shooting from the roadway and taking an antlerless deer without a permit. Only deer with at least one 3-inch antler could be taken this particular season.

After inspecting the fawn deer for a bullet that appeared to have passed through, I loaded the deer in my patrol truck. I then searched the roadway for a possible spent cartridge casing. There it was, shining like a piece of glass along the shoulder—one .308 caliber empty shell casing. Putting the casing in my blaze orange jacket pocket, I drove around the area and eventually into town, confident that this violator would be mine in the next couple of days. I continued my duties throughout the rest of the deer season and on into the winter months, always having in the back of my mind the eventual sighting of the "DEER HUNTER."

Everyone I talked to about this truck and its give-away bug deflector said the same thing: "Yeah, I remember seeing that many times, but I don't know who owns it!" I was still totally sure I would run into him eventually, just because of the number of patrol miles I put on throughout the year.

The winter passed into spring. All the other enforcement duties typical of the seasons—fish run, summer fishing, fall duck hunting activity—passed, without a sight of the elusive pickup truck. Then late fall, knowing full well that the violator had removed his bug screen and that chances were slim I would ever make contact. It now was almost a year from the date of the infraction, the empty casing still rattling around in my coat pocket, and me ramming around town getting equipped and psyched up for the next big deer season. I needed some new gloves and pulled my patrol vehicle into my favorite hardware store. It was a busy place and there was only one parking space along the rows of trucks and cars. I pulled into the remaining spot, and as I looked up at the vehicle parked directly facing me, to my amazement I saw one brown Ford pickup with a bug deflector that read "DEER HUNTER." Soon I saw a young man approach and begin opening the driver's side door. I asked him if I could talk to him for just a minute. He agreed, and immediately I noticed a case gun on a rack in the back window of his truck.

I said, "Sir, I'm Tom, the local conservation officer, and I think you and I have to have a talk."

"About what?"

I said, "First, before we talk, I'd like to have a bet with you."

Now getting more confused, he said, "What kind of bet?"

I said, "I'll bet you the price of a new deer license that I can guess the caliber of that rifle you are carrying in your truck right there." He now was acting totally confused when I said, "I'll bet that's a .308 you're carrying."

"Well, how did you know that?" he said.

"I'll bet it matches this shell casing right here," I said as I pulled the year-old piece of evidence from my pocket.

"What do you mean? How do you know that?"

"Because," I said, "it matches the rifle that you used to shoot an illegal fawn deer last year off of County Road 10, on November 9 at 2:30 P.M. in the afternoon. Now you can lie to me or you can just tell me the truth and save yourself a lot of problems. Did you shoot the deer that I'm referring to with that gun while driving this pickup?"

One of the longest pauses then took place during any interview I've ever done. He looked around, looked at his pickup, looked back at me, looked back at the ground and finally said, "Yeah, I did it!" Those are good words to a conservation officer when knowing full well an admission is the only hope of getting some justice.

You see, there was no direct evidence—no one observing the actual shooting—that would lead to a conviction, other than he admitting to the offense. The witness's statements, the deer, the shell casing—all circumstantial—were probably not enough to prosecute, although that would be up to the county attorney to decide. The defendant walked into the courtroom the following Monday with his mother and pleaded guilty to the taking of an antlerless deer with no permit and shooting from the roadway.

I learned another valuable lesson—*Never give up!!*

NINETEEN
The Corvette Caper

Sometimes I think back to my biggest challenges while enforcing the game and fish laws, and I still shudder at the thoughtlessness and basic stupidity of some of my decisions to throw caution to the wind. Many of my "less-gifted" judgments were a function of youth, combined with a sudden loss of common sense when the adrenaline started to surge. Also, the they-can't-get-away-with-that! attitude that occasionally clouded my rationality while I observed an ongoing violation. "I may have to turn to some unorthodox procedures in the capture, but the capture will take place," was my only thought during many of these predicaments.

One particular incident comes to mind regarding the apprehension of fish poachers. It was in the "hopeless arrest" category and had so little chance of a resolution that the only choice was to employ some drastic methods.

A small winding creek that poured into a large lake north of Grand Rapids always produced a large run of northern pike in the spring of the year. It was also one of the first streams in the area where large fish could be seen, even when ice was still on the lake. As these large pike worked their way upstream, their half-mile trip ended at a 4-foot spillway which stopped their progress. This was a spot that the locals were aware of, and due to its remote location, it was a prime area for the preseason taking of big fish.

However, there was only a narrow one-lane trail accessing the dam-like structure. This made it difficult for anyone who had intentions of acquiring illegal fish to hide from view. For an officer to observe a violation, he would have to hide his patrol vehicle at least a mile away and walk to the site to set up a surveillance position. Of course, any potential violator would have to do the same thing.

I had worked this spot alone at least a dozen times over five years without success. I continued to go back because of the size and quantity of the fish available and because of the evidence I had found of fish being taken in the past. There was never any doubt that this was a poachers' paradise.

One clear cold April night, I drove in and hid my truck like every other time taking up a surveillance spot on a hill above the water. I could hear the fish splashing around in the shallow water so I knew the big fish were making their run and were vulnerable to poaching.

An hour went by . . . then two . . . three, and finally about 1:00 A.M., I could see vehicle lights flashing from side to side along the soggy rutted road below me. Were these just lookers, or was their intention to jump the season on northern pike? It would all come down to how much I could see of their actions and movements and still remain undetected. The car finally stopped at the turn-around and shut off its lights. My binoculars gathered enough light to discern two men walking down to the edge of the water, looking around a minute and then hurrying back to their parked car.

Many times violators will go to a site to learn if there's anything worth taking, leave the area quickly and come back later to do their damage. This appeared to be the case here since they spent so little time watching the fish. I thought it was now or never with these guys. Gotta check them out! Possessing a spear or net near water in the spring of the year was also a violation, so why not save some fish before they could be taken?

I decided to approach the vehicle before it was turned around and see what type of equipment might be inside. I sneaked up through some brush to the passenger side of the small-size car just as they were starting to back up. As the headlights turned, I attempted to hunch down so as not to be seen until I could maneuver to a position on the driver's side. That's when they saw me. Like a deer in the headlights, there I stood, in total view of the two occupants. I had absolutely no choice but to identify myself, approach the vehicle, and check them out.

This is when my poor approach and their illegal intentions became entangled. With a powerful roar of the engine, the car took off in reverse, throwing mud all over me and gaining speed back down the trail. My first thought was, How did they get this little, low-clearance car back here on this awful, muddy, rutted trail? It was a Corvette! I ran toward the front of the bumper but couldn't quite keep up with the car's acceleration, even in reverse. It was miraculous that the driver could keep it on the trail with the wheels spinning and the accelerator to the floor. There was no way he could see where I was, with all his efforts concentrated on getting away. I imagined his buddy screaming at him to go faster, faster, as I was now in the headlights sprinting toward them. At first I didn't think I had a chance to catch the vehicle, and what would I have done with it anyway? One muddy C.O. against two people in a Corvette!

But then the nature of the trail came to my assistance. The conditions of the road had allowed the car to reach its peak reverse speed, but I could keep up with it, and my involuntary reflexes and adrenalin must have then taken control. I jumped on the hood!! Everything unraveled in slow motion. I actually thought, I'm being taken for a ride down a muddy road in the dark at 2:00 A.M., lying on top of a Corvette that's rapidly accelerating in reverse, not even knowing if there's a violation, and having no clue who these people are! This can't be good!

I got a tight grip on the rear of the hood by the wiper blades and just hung on knowing they would eventually have to slow down at a "T" a quarter mile down the road. Probably due to the driver's frustration in failing to detach his extra passenger, he backed off the road out of control. The Corvette landed on the top of a large rut where it got hung up and couldn't move. I jumped off the hood and ran up to the driver's door. Surprisingly, it was unlocked, so I jerked it open and put the rays of my flashlight into the driver's eyes and identified myself, "Conservation Officer! Please get out of the car!"

Luckily, they both complied and stood in front of the headlights as I ordered. I told them that my partners were at the end of the road waiting for more directions, so the two of them had better behave themselves. (We're allowed to lie if it's for our personal protection.) After looking at their identification (I recognized them after I saw their names), I peered into the car's interior.

There it was, a long-handled spear wedged between the seats and the back window. It took quite an effort to remove the implement, which explained why it hadn't been tossed out the window during all the commotion. This was all the evidence that I needed to secure a violation. It also verified my suspicions that these boys had intentions to go home with a fresh fish dinner.

Both perpetrators were quiet and unresponsive and gave me no more trouble (most likely because they really thought they were surrounded), so I just charged them with possessing a spear near waters in the spring. I didn't push the free car ride due to my experience in the local court with respect to other situations like this. (A "failure to stop" or "careless driving" charge would probably have been thrown out.) Sometimes you're just so happy to have the incident over with, incidental charges don't provide any further satisfaction.

A couple more fish saved for the legal people! But only a couple? One has to think about the potential damage spring fish poaching does to the spawning female population, preventing hundreds of next-generation northerns from being available.

TWENTY

The Cluttered Shack

Harsh winters in Northern Minnesota during the early 1970s forced officials to impose severe restrictions on the taking of deer for the next decade. The first-ever ban on antlerless deer, combined with much shorter seasons, changed the character of the traditional nine-day hunt forever.

Many hunters who were accustomed to shooting any deer now had to hone their skills in order to identify a "legal" deer (one with at least a 3-inch polished antler) prior to harvesting. Most sportsmen adjusted well to the new rules, conscious that agreeing to concessions was the only means to increase herd numbers. However, a small group of folks expressed little concern for the deer population by persisting in their illegal behavior.

I was unaware of anything out of the ordinary in a remote area of southern Itasca County until I began receiving anonymous calls from witnesses who saw antlerless deer being transported in the vicinity of County Road 72 during the deer season. After five years of patrolling assorted complaint areas, I began concentrating my efforts along this stretch and its scores of intersecting trails. The more hunters I talked to, the more enlightened I became about probable illegal activity. It appeared that some of the legal hunters were being intimidated and harassed by a particular group of men headquartering at a local bar. Many witnessed illegal deer in possession and intoxicated hunting or experienced being forced off stands and pressured out of prime hunting spots.

The common link seemed to be the drinking establishment at the end of the road. Parked in the rear lot were two large motor homes with extension cords providing electricity from the bar. License identification of those and other vehicles nearby revealed a home base for some hunters from a small southwestern Minnesota town.

I continued to devote many hours patrolling this stretch and checking licenses, some belonging to members of this large hunting party. I learned more about their behavior and attitudes as many of them, through bar talk and gossip from local residents, projected an aversion to law enforcement, especially game wardens!

The following year and first evening of deer season, I put the bar lot under surveillance. Just after sunset, I spotted people moving between the motor homes and a one-room shack on the south edge of the property. Some were carrying boxes; others were drinking and partying.

Convinced this little cabin held some clues to the mystery, I waited until most of the folks had migrated to the bar before I knocked on the door.

"C'mon in," came a shout through the thin walls. Pressing the door slowly forward, I stepped inside and quickly pulled it shut. Standing directly in front of me was a very rotund gentleman sporting a bewildered look. "Oh, hi! I thought it was . . . What can I do for you?"

"Good evening, Sir. My name's Tom, the local game warden. Just wondering how your deer season's going so far. Had any success?"

"Well . . . uh . . . I don't hunt! I just live here . . . I mean, this is my house . . . and you can see . . . well . . . these aren't mine!"

A glance around the tiny living quarters revealed boxes full of fresh meat scattered around the room. Other items included a bloody table covered with tallow scraps, hides and bones lying on the linoleum, a large butcher knife, and—the most unusual sighting—a deer hoof sticking out from under a bed.

"You say these deer parts don't belong to you? Then whose are they?"

Pacing around the little floor space that remained between the cardboard boxes, he anxiously muttered, "I can't tell you that!"

"What do you mean, you can't tell me. You're in big trouble with a house full of unregistered, untagged deer, and you refuse to tell me how they got here or who brought them?"

"Not that I can't," he said. "I won't! They'd hurt me awful bad!"

"They're the boys next door, aren't they? They've been poaching the hell out of this neighborhood, haven't they?"

"That's all I'm going to say!" he shouted, as beads of sweat dripped from his chin. "Do what you have to do . . . I'm not saying another thing!"

"O.K., Sir. We'll talk about that later. Let's see how many deer you have here," I said, as I slowly pulled a fawn from under the bed.

"Should be seven. I've done this for many years. I know it's wrong, but they've got me hooked. I process an average of 22 a year."

"Are any of these deer legal bucks?" I asked.

"None. They're all does and fawns. All illegal!"

"So what did they do . . . hire you to cut them up?"

"They give me booze," he said. "I'm an alcoholic and can't afford the stuff!"

"So who gives you the alcohol? Listen, I'm not after you. I want the boys who are killing all these animals. You help me out and I won't even charge you. You've been used, so getting these guys will be in both our interests."

"You're going to have to arrest me, then, cuz I ain't telling. I can't!!"

I didn't blame him a bit. He was in their pocket!

Besides the butchering mess, the room reeked of garbage and empty liquor bottles. It was easy to feel sorry for this hapless character who lived in conditions unfit for any human being.

He was in total fear, not necessarily due to my presence but from the offensive neighbors who, I was now convinced, would indeed do him harm if he was to inform on them. I needed more information before making any arrests, but I knew the ball was in his court. Without his statement or testimony declaring names and places, any case against those wildlife marauders would be impossible to make.

I continued talking to my defendant about his background, interests and previous employment. He was a decent person whose personal circumstances contributed to his being abused by a bunch of unscrupulous, greedy hunters—and now he was trapped by the fear of retribution. He was forced to take responsibility for the whole mess, and I couldn't help him. There was no doubt that I would have to charge him with illegal possession of the seven deer. If I didn't, and the others discovered my house-call, he might wind up in a deeper dilemma. I also thought that there would be future opportunities to capture these outlaws.

The legal process ran its course, forcing my guy to spend some jail time and to pay a large fine.

He started to confide in me during the next few years, even calling and stopping by occasionally to give me info as he began to feel more comfortable. As a result of his little tips, I was able to arrest two of the bandits for deer shining one late fall evening. A jury found them not guilty, but now they were aware that somebody was watching.

We became good friends, and finally one day he told me that he had separated himself from his outlaw associates. He revealed further information on the methods of operation that were used during the many illegal deer hunts he witnessed.

My informant revealed more about himself as time passed. He worked previously for the Wisconsin DNR as a fisheries employee and possessed numerous outdoor skills. Six years after this incident, he finally succumbed to the alcoholism that plagued him so much of his life.

Parts of seven illegal deer found the first night of season inside a one-room cabin.

TWENTY ONE
The Bag Bears

In my opinion, black bears are funny animals! Maybe not hilariously funny—it's just that the subject of bears seems to spawn laughter.

A good number of human-bear contacts that I've witnessed as a game warden, including damage complaints, developed into a humorous contest, the bear prevailing more often than not.

The more I dealt with black bears, the greater my admiration and respect for these mostly misunderstood, intelligent and gentle creatures. It took a great deal of time for me to educate people about the passiveness of an animal that carries such a naturally menacing appearance. Sometimes just the presence of a bear would intimidate people enough for them to call in a report. Dealing with these complaints supplied the fodder for many wacky and amusing events.

In earlier years, it was not uncommon for game wardens to tranquilize problem bears. Mostly done in urban areas, darting was a last resort and only employed after live-trapping or harassing failed. Most likely upon my arrival, the bear, and sometimes a female's cubs, would be slumbering on a tree branch, reluctant to come down because of the assembly of gawking people or the yapping of the neighborhood dogs from below. Once conditions reached this level, sedating the animal for removal was the preferred option.

Two lively episodes involved the transportation of 20-pound balls of dozing fur to a healthier and happier location far from town.

The first incident found me heading north of Grand Rapids with a semicomatose black mass stuffed inside a tightly cinched Duluth pack. Like earlier uneventful trips, I assumed the little cub would snooze the next twenty miles to the release site.

About 4 miles into the journey, I heard rustling behind me on the backseat of the four-door sedan. A quick look revealed the bag stirring like a miniature boxer trying to punch his way out. Not to worry, I thought, since the largest air gap was only 2 inches square, and the bear would be extremely groggy for at least the next thirty minutes.

Traffic was fairly heavy on the shoulderless state highway when I glanced in the rear-view mirror, which revealed two beady red eyes restlessly staring back at me. The black bundle of hair and muscle was propped in the back window ledge, and it looked fired up! How in the world could it have possibly escaped from that bag? I said to myself. Time for plan B!

One setback already; I had no plan B or any other plan in the alphabet for that matter. I recognized, however, the need for the bear and I to part company immediately. I'm sure the bear was having the same idea; where's the quickest exit? Operating a motor vehicle with a panting, toothy animal crawling around behind your back creates a tingly sense of dread.

If I slammed on the brakes at 50 miles per hour, the momentum would catapult the critter forward, right into the front seat. If I slowed down gradually, the greater the opportunity for the vicious little beast to gnaw on my neck or bite my face off.

I pressed the brake pedal to the floor, slammed the car in park, and vaulted from the driver's side, hoping to avoid getting

scrunched by oncoming traffic. As the car skidded to a squealing stop in the middle of the highway, I jumped from the burnt
rubber tainted confines, leaving the door wide open, just as the
bear scrambled over the front seat. It then crawled up on the
dash and sat, staring out the rear window and clutching the
steering wheel with its fat little paws. And there I stood on the
center line, oblivious to approaching traffic and pondering my
next move.

Now that my vehicle had been hijacked by the feisty little
bruin, my options were limited: I could wait until its instincts
told it to flee, or I could return and coax it out. As a curious
audience gathered around the scene, a familiar voice rose above
the hubbub. "What seems to be the dilemma, Tom?" It was the
county sheriff, who by chance was behind me on the highway
when I ground to a stop.

"Well, Russ, I've got this extremely nasty passenger that
refuses to get out of my car. Mind giving me a hand here?" As
a former game warden himself, a situation like this wasn't all
that unique.

"Yeah. I'll open the passenger door and maybe he'll jump out."

Novel idea, I thought. I could have done that myself if I had
retained my wits.

The spirited beastie now saw the light. With two leaps, one
onto the seat and the other out the door, he scampered directly
into the thick stand of jack pine along the ditch.

"One more bear release," I shouted at the onlookers as I
jumped in my patrol car and reached over to pull the opposite
door shut. "Just happened to be a few miles short of the
intended site."

As we were leaving, Russ offered, "Ya might want to fasten
the bag a little tighter next time, Tom."

The second bear-liberating disaster was almost a carbon-copy of the first. If I would have taken the pack-tightening advice to heart, I could have avoided another BBR (Botched Bear Release)!

It started once again with a sleepy cub placed in a tightly drawn packsack lying in the box of my pickup truck. This time, I pulled the straps an extra notch tighter to prevent another bear escape. Not even a mouse could squeeze through the cracks this time!

This last thought took a mere ten minutes to prove false. As I crossed the viaduct south of town, a peek at my rear-view mirror jolted me. The bear cub had not only gotten out, but it was standing erect, facing the rear with its paws resting on the tailgate at 55 miles per hour. How could the drug have worn off that fast? The bear's probably thinking the same thing: I'm not tired any more and I want out of this speed box.

My second thought concerned the driver directly behind me. What exactly was going through his mind as he stared at a bear glaring back at him. I'll never know. That worry didn't last long as the minute I started slowing down, the little black ball leaped from the back of the truck onto the hilly shoulder and rolled through the cable guardrail and down a 20-foot embankment to the sandy beach below. With no place to pull off, I stopped in the roadway to determine the poor animal's condition. I knew I was creating a small traffic jam, but I had to run down and check for life.

I didn't get even halfway down the embankment before the tough little brute shook the sand off its fur and galloped full-speed down the beach, directly toward a restaurant. Up the two flights of stairs it dashed, past the dining room windows and disappeared around the corner of the building.

Running back to my truck, I addressed a few slightly irate drivers who asked what the heck was going on. "Another nuisance bear release," I declared with all the professionalism I could muster. "Just stepped out a little early, that's all. But thanks for asking!" I then nonchalantly jumped in my truck and drove south thinking about the next sleepy-bear transport. This one would be sealed inside a 55-gallon drum!

One of the sedated cub bears that later awakened a little too early.

TWENTY TWO
The Failed Flee

Sometimes it's difficult for good people to evade the truth without radiating guilty clues. Body movements, facial expressions, tones of voice, or lack of eye contact are just a few indicators of deceptive conduct. Quickly recognizing these traits can help law enforcement officers make better on-the-spot decisions when dealing with a possible violator, especially when the window of opportunity is brief.

Game wardens are forced repeatedly to make hasty assessments. There is so little time and so many details to analyze during a short boat inspection or hunter check! An officer just relies on his training and instincts.

Late fall fishing is superb on Lake Winnibigoshish. Many fishermen plan their annual vacations to include this cool and colorful time of the year. Compliance with fishing laws is normally very good. Nevertheless, a few citizens will occasionally yield to the greed factor and take advantage of the premium harvest.

The evening was warm and pleasant for late September, a far cry from the previous day's wind and rain that blew most fishermen off the lake. As I stood at the launch site of a public access on Cutfoot Lake, I questioned whether the fish were biting after such a turbulent twenty-four hours; often they remain inactive following turbulent weather.

The boats started returning at dusk showing their red and green bow lights as they approached the floating dock. Surprisingly, the first three boats of fishermen had their live-wells full of fish, many containing near limits.

The last craft to tie up was an 18-footer holding three eager-to-get-going anglers. As I knelt alongside, I asked them if their luck was as good as some of the others I had checked earlier and told them I'd seen a lot of nice fish already.

"Yeah, We've done all right," one of them mumbled as he walked quickly past me to retrieve his truck and trailer. I asked the other two, now standing on the pier, if I could inspect their catch. They both agreed as I stepped down and opened the live-well cover.

I counted 17 walleyes, one under the limit for three people. I thanked them and watched while they packed up and then drove from the lot.

As the red taillights disappeared around the corner, I wrestled with a tiny pang of unease. I couldn't put my finger on it, but something seemed awry with this group. Maybe it was an inflection in a voice or a dialogue shift that pressed me to shadow them. Something almost subliminal put me behind their vehicle as they pulled onto the main highway northbound.

Following at a long distance, I strained to keep an eye on the trailer lights for the next 10 miles until the truck pulled into a convenience store. Five minutes later they left the parking lot and proceeded 15 miles in the opposite direction, circling the gas pumps of a restaurant and heading west onto a blacktop county road. It all appeared to be some form of evasive action; so as far as I was concerned, they had just become suspects. Suspects of what, I wasn't sure, but I was now more confident that I was on an enforcement mission.

In the meantime, I had driven passed the restaurant parking lot until I was out of sight. I turned around after cutting my lights and soon pulled in behind the westbound rig. Following on their tail the next 4 miles, I saw the intensity of the unit's brake lights go on as it turned north toward the only residence on a dead-end road 4 miles ahead—a resort!

I knew the owner and was secure in the fact that he was a big enforcement supporter. If there would be a need for assistance or cooperation, there could be nobody better, even if these folks turned out to be his clients.

Driving in the black of night at a steady pace using only the taillights ahead for guidance, our short sojourn finally ended in front of the resort's fish cleaning/garage combination. A small yard light partially lit the scene but I could still hide in the shadows as I exited my truck. "Hey, you guys, over here. Can I talk to you a minute?" I hollered from the rear of the boat trailer.

All three spun around and peered into the darkness. "Who's there? What do you want?"

"Game Warden again. I just have one more matter I'd like to clear up," I said as I moved toward the light to expose my uniform.

I could instantly detect sagging shoulders and downcast gaits as they approached. "Just thought you might possibly have some more fish other than what I saw earlier. Maybe in your cabin. Is that possible?"

Barely audible, one member of the entourage blurted, "No, I don't think so."

"O.K. If you don't mind, I'll follow you to your cabin just to make sure."

One of the men remained at the truck while the other two led me to the farthest cottage along the shore of Lake Winnibigoshish. Into the cabin we all went where they showed me the interior of the freezer compartment of the refrigerator.

"You see? Nothing here!"

"How about the refrigerator?" I asked as I slowly opened the door. The inside was totally devoid of food EXCEPT for one large plastic bag of fish fillets. I removed the plastic sack and put it on a table to count the contents. Two, four, six, nine, fifteen . . . fifty-eight. That made twenty-nine walleyes total—and combined with the fish in the boat, well over the possession limit for three people.

The third gentleman joined the others while I issued summonses and instructed them on their options. Gentlemen they were. Three of the nicest guys who just didn't know when to stop. They apologized and seemed to accept my presence as a positive encounter. None had ever been checked by a warden before, and everyone most likely assumed there were no obstacles in taking as many fish as they wanted.

This was confirmed by my resort–owner friend who had a difficult time accepting these guys as fish poachers. "Of all the groups I get at my resort during the year, I would have suspected these guys the least. I've learned a lot about your type of work," he said. "I still trust most people, but I watch just a little closer now."

The next day my resort friend and I had a good discussion about the importance of body language and verbal clues when trying to determine honesty and sincerity among his customers. We decided there was little difference between our jobs and the folks we deal with on a daily basis; most are great, a few are not. We also agreed that whatever that little birdie in the recesses of the mind is called—intuition, a good hunch, instinct or a sixth sense—take it seriously, it can make a tremendous difference in the positive outcomes of hard to define enforcement situations.

TWENTY THREE
The Patient Hunter

Big buck contests are scattered throughout deer hunting country in the fall. Usually they are sponsored by nonprofit organizations, sportsmen's clubs or retail outlets promoting their businesses. Entry into the contests is just a matter of purchasing a ticket prior to the animal being taken. The bucks or does, depending on the type of contest, are weighed and registered, followed by cash or other forms of prizes awarded at the end of the season to the shooter of the heaviest deer. The contests can include deer taken by either archery or firearms, with honors presented for each category.

Not that this style of fund-raising is a bad thing, but conservation officers have been hesitant to totally embrace the concept owing to abuse among some of the contestants. Actually, C.O.'s become very uneasy when there is a contest involving payment or recognition for the taking of game or fish. Fishing contests seem to be the most exploited. There's more than one story about contestants attempting to enter frozen fish. Human greed and bragging factors start to overwhelm some people who will resort to illegal methods to satisfy these desires. The following accounts are examples depicting this type of behavior.

I developed a habit of monitoring photos in the local newspaper with a large buck or big fish. I enjoyed examining the names of the persons with the big grins behind their trophies and attempted to relate the names or locations to earlier poaching cases.

One October day I spotted a photo of an individual with whom I had previous contact; in fact, his entire family was rumored to eat fresh venison all year. Here he was, kneeling next to a buck deer, with bow and arrow in hand. The hunter's quote in the caption read: "Anyone can get a deer this way. You just have to be patient."

My first reaction was amusement, "This guy doesn't have the patience, let alone the ambition, to take a deer with a bow and arrow!" It was a, What's-wrong-with-this-picture reaction—just a thought that eventually passed into my mental log of mini-facts. I had cut out the piece and shoved it into a folder, thinking it would most likely never be retrieved again.

Twelve months later, almost to the day, a late night patrol steered a fellow officer and me to a gravel road in the center of Balsam Township. A quiet cool night, conditions were not unlike many other late fall evenings when the deer could be found feeding on the remnants of green grasses along this remote forest trail. This night the deer were abundant, feeding from ditch to ditch far in front of the headlights. Occasionally one would stand motionless as we drove slowly by, its eyes reflecting like tiny mirrors.

Any vehicle moving at 1:00 A.M. was suspect and would be observed for hints of mischief. Slow, wandering motion, sporadic brake lights, or an older model vehicle were all indications that the driver's intentions might be more than just a joy ride.

As we turned around to follow a vehicle that had already passed by, we deliberated as to the chance of being recognized as an enforcement vehicle. Now running "black" with our headlights off and trailing a couple car lengths behind, it was instantly clear to us that the driver was watching the deer. The brake lights, the slow speed—all the indicators were visible; but what were his intentions? Looking or taking? We would have to follow him until our suspicions were confirmed.

After two miles of slow-speed driving, the brake lights flashed again, only this time they remained lit while the car slowly came to a full stop. Pulling directly behind the rear bumper, we waited for a sign of movement inside. In less than a minute, the interior light came on and a shadowy figure emerged from the driver's side. The darkness of the night completely hid our car as I slowly opened my door. With our dome light cut off, I was able to maneuver around the passenger side of the suspect's vehicle.

As I knelt beside the right front fender, I could see a deer staring back at the headlights and the suspect kneeling between the lights aiming a bow and arrow at full draw in the deer's direction. Very cautiously, I crept under the right headlight and up behind the man's shoulders. The instant I laid my hands on the back of his neck, TWANG, the arrow released from the bow as the man froze in a terrified state of panic. "What the . . . what the . . . geeeez . . . holy . . . I . . . !"

I told him to stay calm and slowly get to his feet as I gently held him in place and checked for other weapons. "Easy," I said. "You're under arrest for shining deer. Just turn around and put your hands on the car hood." Totally cooperative, he reached his arms straight out and then back behind as I applied the handcuffs.

So far, I had not identified the offender until I removed an I.D. from his wallet and held his driver's license up in front of my flashlight. I recognized the name and immediately looked into the man's face to confirm it. Shouting at my partner, I said, "You won't believe who we just nabbed. It's 'Mr. Patience,' the archery hunter in the newspaper last year!"

"Unbelievable! Well, you know what they say; what goes around . . . !"

Further search of the car uncovered a current $5.00 big buck contest ticket purchased five days earlier.

There are special arrests where the level of satisfaction is a notch above the others. This was one!! Especially when I was able to frame last year's newspaper article alongside this year's conviction notice.

Another case occurred in the Swan River area, 20 miles southeast of Grand Rapids. The same general factors were present: a slow-moving pickup truck rattling down a remote gravel road early in the morning. My neighboring officer had been tailing the vehicle for a short time and radioed to me that he may need help in making a stop on a couple of suspects who were using a handheld spotlight.

Before I had covered the 20 miles to the general location, he hollered that he had them stopped and everything was under control. Arriving at the scene, I assisted in the usual matters of the arrests and interrogation. Both were charged with deer shining. The two young men involved had been hitting a number of fields with a spotlight and eventually parked their truck crossways in the road; all the time their movements were being scrutinized by my partner.

It was decided to seize the vehicle, inventory the contents and call for a wrecker. The evidence clearly showed their intentions; a cross-bow with broadhead shafts and a four-power scope attached, was lying on the front seat next to a warm spotlight. Even though no deer was taken, this equipment comprised everything necessary to sustain deer-shining convictions. Searching further inside the cab, a large yellow ticket was found attached to the driver's visor. It read: "Big Buck Archery Contest, Bovey, Minnesota," the purchase date being the previous day!

This is yet another example of a few bad apples taking advantage of their fellow sportsmen by using illegal methods to satisfy their greed and ego.

TWENTY FOUR
The Crafty Netters

Numerous techniques exist by which fish are taken illegally in Minnesota. However, the gill net has always ranked at the top of a fish poacher's list of unlawful tools. Spring-spawning walleyes and northern pike, as they concentrate in the shallows of local lakes and rivers, are especially vulnerable to this contrivance.

The most common style of gill net, occasionally referred to as a "square hook," consists of a 100-foot by 3-foot linkage of square nylon mesh, each square measuring one and three quarter inches. Floats attached the full length on one side and weights along the other allow the net to be suspended horizontally at various depths. Anchors and ropes are attached to the ends to keep it in place and make it retrievable. The diameter of the mesh allows the head of the fish to enter just past the gill-cover where it becomes entangled and trapped. Due to the effectiveness of this design, even removing the fish by hand can be difficult.

Minnesota has a number of specially regulated lakes where gill netting is permitted for commercial harvesting of gamefish or for the taking of nongame species such as whitefish and tullibees.

A gill net is not an unusual possession for many residents of Itasca County. The majority of them are used for legal activities; however, a few end up in the hands of those who intend to abuse the fish resource.

Over four years I received tales of a netting operation on Sugar Lake that had been continuing for a generation. The initial reports only involved bits and pieces from a couple residents of the lake who had received the netted fish as gifts. One particular lady notified me of her concern over the walleye population being depleted by a neighbor living down the shoreline. According to her, this individual would gill net every spring and accumulate so many fish that they would be given away to the neighbors.

At first, I assumed this would be an easy arrest, given the name of the perpetrator had already been supplied. It didn't take me long to discover that this was anything but the case! Countless hours of cold, tiresome surveillance proved fruitless.

Sugar Lake is a large, round, clear body of water southwest of Grand Rapids that gives up its ice later than most. Many of the older homes are perched on a bluff along the north shoreline of sandy beaches with a lake-bottom that deepens very gradually–a perfect environment for late-spawning walleyes!

One of these long-time residents, a man in his late forties, was the focus of my scrutiny. All the evidence suggested a late night/early morning scheme, involving at least two people. Another key point linked the placement of the net to the lights being left on at the residence. This was critical because it was difficult to approach the place, in order to survey the surroundings and attached shoreline, without being detected. Most every night during the height of the run, the lights were off. Many times other officers and I would observe the site for hours, but to no avail. If the lights were off when we arrived, we would wait for activity until 2:00 A.M. Lights were sometimes on early in the evening but were always shut off by midnight.

It was very frustrating, because the information seemed very credible and the conditions were perfect. The informant would call every year and inquire as to why this person wasn't apprehended because of the illegal fish she was continuing to receive.

In the fifth spring, I got a call one evening from a person with a questionable game and fish reputation, who was quite well known as an area minnow dealer. He was very brusque with the information: "I know a guy on Sugar Lake who will be netting tomorrow night. I want him caught."

"Hold on before you hang up," as I shouted out the probable suspect's name.

"Yeah, that's him all right, and there are more involved."

"Just one more second," I pleaded. "The word is that he nets only when the lights are on in his kitchen. Is that right?"

"You've been led astray, my boy," he said. "The lights are always off. Off! Never a light on anywhere!! It's yours from here on!" He hung up.

Considering my informant's reputation, I immediately thought the call was either a setup or it was too good to be true. I wondered if a feud had developed between my caller and those people at Sugar Lake.

After all these years, had I finally got the right information? Had I been just sitting out there all those dark nights with the cabin lights off, and all the while the net had already been set? I wasn't quite sure what to think, but I knew I had to get into high gear and prepare for the next night's surveillance.

With no officers immediately available for assistance, I asked a civilian if he would like to sit on a watch late in the evening and possibly into the next morning. After he agreed, we set up on a hill next to the residence. There was no moon, leaving the stars to provide the only light. It was so dark that I could barely distinguish my partner sitting right next to me. The night was windless and clear with a temperature of 40 degrees. Three-quarters of the lake was ice covered, and the lights in the kitchen were off; the setting was perfect!

The house sat on a hill about 100 feet from the shoreline. Sitting 200 feet east of the house, it was difficult for us to see any movement other than the slight rippling of the stars reflecting off the water.

About 11:30 P.M., while gazing out on the lake with my binoculars, I saw some movement; no noise, just a slight variation in the shadows at the water's edge. A concentrated inspection finally revealed the faint outline of a human form. There was no noise, only a gray figure moving from the water toward the hill. At that point, my binoculars failed to follow any further progress. Nothing! Just a continued quiet with only the distant sound of seagulls splashing and squawking.

However, the vague sighting was enough to call in some help. I ran back to my hidden patrol unit and called two other officers, advising them of my location and that a night of surveillance lay ahead. My two neighboring C.O.'s arrived quickly, and I told them the circumstances. They had both helped on this case before, so they knew the terrain and with whom we might be dealing.

The minutes and hours passed anxiously for us. We were sure of nothing, not even that a net had been placed. Two o'clock turned slowly into 3:00 A.M. Intently watching the shoreline around 3:30, I suddenly saw the shadows of two persons shifting on the beach. We became alert and decided to wait until one or both entered the water so as to give us an advantage. We then lost sight of one outline for a couple of minutes, while the other profile continued to stand near the water. At last, about 20 feet out in the lake, we noticed a silhouette approaching the sandy beach. This was the crucial moment; we'll take them now!

As we increased our pace to a quick stride, all four of us engaged our flashlights about 30 feet from shore. That was when the situation began to deteriorate. The first thing I noticed was a large man, in chest waders, standing in the water up to his knees dragging a net. At the same time a fellow officer shouted, "There's three!" I quickly looked around and saw the officer chasing a person up the hill toward the cabin. I glanced back at my man in the water who failed to do what I requested of him. "Conservation Officer, stay right there where you are! Don't move! Put the net down!"

It's certainly not that he didn't hear me; he just had no desire to be captured! The hulk turned toward the deeper water and waded out as fast as he could—to his waist, over his waders, and then up to his neck, continuing to swim and dragging the net behind him. He moved so fast that none of us were able to stop him without ourselves going for a cold dip. At that moment it wasn't a huge concern because nobody could last long in that freezing, ice-laden water. He'll be heading back this way real soon, we thought.

We were wrong. As the other officers were trying to round up and control the other two suspects, with my flashlight focused I continued to watch my guy as he swam farther and farther out into the darkness, still dragging the net. Barely visible by now, the floating shape started heading west, parallel to the shoreline. This is impossible, I thought to myself. How can a human being stand the vicious cold this long? And what's he going to do next?

Suddenly safety became our primary concern. This man wasn't going to survive unless we got him out of that water. Shouting had no effect, so our only chance was to go out and return him to shore. Two of us grabbed an overturned boat and rowed out in the direction of the dark wake which had already advanced 100 yards down the shoreline. Rowing up next to him, we told him to give up this nonsense and get in our boat before he froze to death. I held out an oar and told him to grab it. Having sunk the net somewhere behind him, he was now able to use both hands to pull the oar from my grip and throw it into the darkness far from the boat. It was becoming more and more obvious that this was somebody who hadn't the slightest intention of surrendering.

Now we had only one oar and little chance of grasping this first-class marathoner in full waders while we were still in the boat. Our partners on shore knew little of our predicament but continued to follow our movements with their flashlights. With the remaining oar, we maneuvered to shore and joined the others in tracking the man's incredible swimming display.

Finally, after a quarter of a mile, the supercharged violator changed his direction 90 degrees and swam toward the beach. With lights trained on his movements, I waded out to him with another officer and attempted to take him into custody—not so easy with an unwilling suspect in three feet of water! Clutching the back of his neck, I instantly found myself thrown on my back into the chilling water. This guy was pumped! My assistant found himself in the same dilemma when he made contact, and this was a man carrying a hundred pounds of water in his waders! C'mon now! There are four of us. But what happens when he reaches land and acquires some footing? I thought.

There was only one solution to save everybody from further struggle. I would have to mace him. Wrong again! A full canister of mace had zero effect on this adrenaline-drenched Leviathan. Emptying the can in his face just made him a little meaner—it failed to stop his forward progress and had no effect on his strength. Stumbling out of the water onto the sandy shore followed by two water-logged, bewildered C.O.'s, he decided to drag himself down the beach toward his residence with water spewing from his waders and sand spurting in all directions. Now there were four of us all over him; one on his neck, one around each leg and another grabbing his right arm. Not a pretty scene for an officer training film! We were only able to force him from his knees to his stomach with a tremendous amount of weight and downward pressure. Once flat, he again tried to get up and crawl through the sand until his head was buried and his air supply exhausted. I'd seen adrenaline do its magic before, but nothing at this intensity. Handcuffs were eventually applied and our behemoth was marched the quarter mile to a squad car to warm up.

My next thought was fixed on the state of the other two net-ters. One of the officers said, "At least we're two out of three. One of them wouldn't respond to a request to halt and escaped into the darkness."

Just after sunrise, the net was retrieved in 20 feet of water and found loaded with walleyes and northern pike, the evidence needed to guarantee a solid conviction.

The $500 fine had little effect on our water monster, but the fifteen days in confinement just about put him over the edge according to the jailers who had to baby-sit him; he had a diffi-cult time being restrained in such a small space.

Often, the rationale given for putting up such a struggle is the dreadful thought of losing social status among peers. They are no longer embraced as heroes, as the "big poacher" who defies the laws and barters illegal fish to his buddies. Failure to round up the entire trio was a disappointment, but I hoped this high-profile arrest would be a strong deterrent on any future ille-gal netting of Sugar Lake.

This tub of large northern pike was confiscated following an illegal netting escapade.

TWENTY FIVE
The Caged Critter

The value of fur-bearer animal skins, such as beaver, otter, raccoon, mink and muskrat, has plummeted since the heyday of the '60s and '70s. This is largely due to an ever-increasing anti-trapping movement and the dramatic shifts in raw fur demands throughout the world. Thirty years ago, it was not unusual for a motivated trapper to net thousands of dollars by the end of the season after selling the hides to local fur buyers or shipping them to Canadian auction houses. Today, one can only hope to break even after the expenses of gas and supplies. The professional trapper who could totally support himself from this sport is now virtually extinct.

The larger fisher, and its smaller cousin the pine marten, are medium-size, bushy-tailed carnivores of the weasel family. The brownish-colored pine marten is the size of an average house cat weighing about 2½ pounds. The fisher can weigh up to 10 pounds and is dark brown or black. These rarely seen furbearers, both legally protected in Minnesota, began expanding their range, and by the mid-1970s were increasingly caught by mistake in traps set for other legal animal species. The rising population of fisher prompted game authorities to establish the first season for trapping in 1977, allowing one per year. The marten season followed a few years later. Today the numbers are high enough to justify the taking of five in combination.

Those years prior to an open season, a prime female fisher hide could bring $275 on the black market. Incidents of unlawfully possessed fishers and rumors of illicit sales alerted Northern Minnesota game wardens to the existence of illegal trafficking of these prized animals.

An anonymous call pointed me toward two acres of woods alongside a one-story bungalow in Lawrence Lake Township. Allegedly, a dark weasel-like animal had been spotted moving about inside a wire mesh cage 100 feet south of the residence. The only living things that I thought matched the description were a fisher or maybe a house cat. Possession of a fisher was in the gross-misdemeanor class of violations, so I quickly went to investigate along with another officer.

Parking a distance away and crawling through hazel brush to the back of the cage, we peaked around the corner and caught a glimpse of a stressed fisher pacing from side to side.

The caller was accurate in his description, but before confronting the owner, we chose to back off and talk to the county attorney about obtaining a search warrant for the rest of the premises.

A couple of hours later, armed with permission to search, we knocked on the door of the house and were greeted by an apprehensive young lady who said her husband would be home from work in half an hour.

"We're conservation officers," I said. "We have a search warrant for your home and outbuildings, but I would rather wait until your husband returns. Would it be okay if we stepped inside?" (I didn't want him to see us as he drove up, and I wanted to keep an eye on her to prevent any phone calls or destruction of potential evidence.)

"Sure. C'mon in. It shouldn't be too long."

Her increased pacing and fretful demeanor made the next fifteen minutes very uncomfortable until her husband bounced up the steps and walked in the door.

"What are you guys doing here?" he said cautiously.

"We couldn't help notice the critter outside in your cage, and we're here to conduct a search for more contraband. We'd appreciate your cooperation and assistance."

He nodded awkwardly and said nothing as I handed him a copy of the warrant and read him the Miranda warning.

He seemed less anxious than his wife and finally mumbled, "Where do you want to look first? We might as well start downstairs. I don't have any more fisher."

I told his wife to accompany the three of us to the basement as we all descended the narrow, dimly lit stairwell. A musky grain-bin smell greeted us as we stepped into the one-room area. Until my pupils adjusted, I wasn't quite sure what I was staring at. As details began to focus, I discerned two large carcasses hanging from the floor joists. The semi-coagulated pools of blood beneath the two deer confirmed their freshness. "So what's the story on these?" I asked.

"Well, Tom, isn't worth lyin' to ya. Shot 'em last night in the driveway."

To the left of the deer was a huge pile of stalks stacked almost to the ceiling. My mind was stuck in the illegal game mode and wasn't yet prepared for this sight—the entire quarter of the cellar was taken up with 8-foot-long stems of freshly harvested marijuana!

Further searching downstairs uncovered nothing more illegal. But now the upstairs became a priority. Ensuring that our two somber defendants were controlled at all times, we proceeded with a full search of cupboards and containers.

It took little time to uncover the intentions of these two people; they were not only game and fur poachers but also local processors and distributors of drugs. Brick after brick of ready-made hashish tumbled out of the kitchen cupboards along with scales, measuring tools and packaging paraphernalia. With 65 2-by-3-inch squares of concentrated illegal dope, this was by no means a small operation.

The search continued to the bedroom where 18 handguns were found scattered in different holds around the room; some, come to find out later—stolen!

Felony possession of stolen property, felony possession of drugs with intent to sell, gross-misdemeanor possession of a fisher and misdemeanor charges of taking two deer during closed season—all a function of one caller's concern about "a little black creature"!

Some major plea bargaining leading to a guilty plea resulted in the imposition of a six-month jail sentence and a five-year probationary period for the husband.

Not all poachers are big time criminals, but many criminals poach.

TWENTY SIX
The Paddling Pursuit

For a mid-October afternoon, the lowering sun was still casting enough warmth to penetrate the backs of our camouflage jackets as we gazed eastward across the huge beds of wild rice. My young student partner and I had just arrived at a remote canoe access on the Bowstring River to check duck hunting activity. Immediately as we stepped from our truck, the blasts of hunters' shotguns echoed across the river's half-mile width. Standing amidst the 3-foot stalks of rice, we could barely detect the open channel running through the midpoint of this vast green and brown sea of vegetation. The 4-mile river separating Bowstring Lake from Big Sand Lake was so choked with growth that a motorboat's prop would soon become encased in stems, bringing it to a stop.

As we gazed across the aquatic field, we sighted three separate hunting groups crouched in blinds and quietly scanning the orange sky for duck formations. Sporadic flocks of ring-bills or mallards would swoop toward the decoys only to be scattered by gunfire, most often missing its mark. Occasionally a bird would plummet followed instantly by the distant thumping report.

As the close of shooting hours approached, two groups began disbanding, climbing into their boats to retrieve decoys and begin the journey home. The last two hunters remained in place, their brown caps barely visible through the binoculars.

The first illegal volley of shots broke the stillness about five minutes after sunset. Strings of ducks were swarming all around us, settling into the pockets of rice to begin their overnight rest. "Let's get our canoe in the water right now!" I directed. "Appears these guys aren't going to quit."

The frequency of the hollow booms increased while we hurriedly loaded our small craft with essential gear: packsacks, paddles, life jackets, flashlights, portable radio and a handheld spotlight wired to a 12-volt car battery. The lengthening shadows had already slid into full dusk, blurring the distant suspects to vague outlines, but the sustained gunfire cued us in to their position.

As the aluminum canoe slid into the weedy grayness for the half-mile paddle, we assumed an over-limit had already been taken along with the confirmed violation of shooting after closed hours. It was now a matter of creeping slowly in their direction to get as close as possible before being detected. We sliced through the first quarter mile of rice until we gained the 50-foot-wide open channel, where we quietly paddled upstream hunched forward, keeping our profile just below the vertical rice stems.

Now opposite the blind, we cautiously entered the last quarter mile of stubborn vegetation. After the shooting had ceased, I peered over the thin shafts to make out the two hunters picking up decoys and tossing them into their motorboat. If we could get just a little closer, escape wouldn't even be an option if they make a run for it, I thought. Even if they do have a motor.

The darkness was our ally now. With only a hundred yards to go, it looked like a done deal. Our paddle tempo increased, the canoe lurching forward after each determined stroke. As we achieved top velocity, the boat's stern-man spotted our intense advance behind him. "Game Warden . . . hold up there . . . stay put please . . . we're going to check you out!"

Staring directly at us, the startled man at the motor promptly engaged the forward throttle, spewing black muck and assorted plant life all over our bow. "STOP! GAME WARDEN!!" I yelled with a commanding tone. "GAME WARDEN. PLEASE SHUT DOWN!"

These two boys not only had no intent of halting, but their goal now was to put as much distance between us as possible until they reached open water. Their 5-horse outboard could then propel them to freedom, never to be seen again.

My bow-man was a young, strapping individual. "Just keep stroking," I directed him. "Pull . . . pull . . . pull," I yelled. "Keep going . . . keep going . . . they don't have a chance in this rice. Look, their motor is clogging already. Keep paddling . . . faster pace . . . stroke . . . stroke . . . stroke . . . we just about got em!"

We could see the operator tipping his motor up and quickly pulling the weeds off the prop. One pull and back they churned into the thick twisted stalks . . . their motor groaning at full speed through the tangled swirls of rice. We had come within four feet of grasping the transom until the little engine blasted them forward again.

"Keep paddling while I get the spotlight on them," I hollered as I fumbled for the snarled cord and tiny switch. "They're going to clog up again. I know we can catch them!" As optimistic as my theory seemed, I found I couldn't paddle and focus the light simultaneously. My partner was exhausted and the rays would only illuminate the backs of their heads. We were losing ground and their channel of escape was only yards away.

Then the 14-foot boat stopped one more time to remove debris from its motor's prop.

"This is our last chance," I yelled. "Give'er everything you've got." I knew my buddy had been going flat out. I was more than aware that residual adrenaline was the only thing keeping him going. He wanted these guys as badly as I did!

This time we drew within an arm's length of the spitting motor. Just one more foot . . . one last all-out exertion from my oxygen-starved arms, and we'll have em! I watched ahead as my hyperventilating co-worker made one last lunge for the fleeing vessel. Stretching his form out over the left gunwale, a fully extended open hand fell short by inches as the craft pulled slowly away. The two men continued rocking themselves front-ward trying to gain a trifle more forward momentum. The tactic seemed to be working.

"O.K . . . O.K . . . Lemme try the light again . . . see if we can I.D. these jokers." I lit up the side of the boat with the 1.5 million candle-power flood as it slid out of the rice-bed into the open water of the river channel. I still couldn't identify any useful features. Our depleted bodies sat in silence studying the elusive prey as it disappeared into foggy obscurity.

"We're not done yet," I said. I reached in and snatched the portable radio from my wet packsack. "K135 to Itasca County . . . K135 to Itasca County . . . Do you have a deputy near the Bowstring bridge?"

"About ten minutes away, Tom. Whatya got?"

In a fatigued voice, I asked, "Get to the bridge ASAP. Lookin for a southbound duck-boat with motor . . . two guys . . . I'm two miles downstream heading that way in a canoe."

About ten minutes later, the deputy came back. "Nothing in sight . . . must have got through before I arrived. I'll meet you at the bridge."

Further searching that evening, including shoreline cabins downstream, uncovered no further evidence or signs of the fugitives.

An "Oh-so-close" unsuccessful capture like this leaves a residue of frustration that takes a very long time to overcome. But realistically, taking a look at the big picture, it was only a few ducks . . . a minor waterfowl violation—and you can't catch them all.

It still hurts though . . . .

TWENTY SEVEN
The Canine Creep

Most of the rules for legally taking fish are nothing more than restrictions the state has imposed to create a "fair chase" climate. Or, the state might extend the number of recreational hours available to harvest a limited resource. In other words, the manner and equipment used to take fish is just as important a factor as the number of fish allowed. These regulations together help maintain a degree of equality and fairness among the thousands of fishermen who compete in the catching.

A stick of dynamite used as a fishing device is illegal everywhere, but taking fish with a multi-hook "trot line" is an accepted method in many states. Some allow "overnight" set lines while others deem it unlawful. Even types of baits, live or artificial, and hooks, barbed or barbless, vary between states and even countries. What is judged to be fair and ethical depends on the particular locale and how the resource is managed.

In Minnesota, open-water fishing with more than one line is illegal on inland lakes–two are allowed through the ice. The reason for the rule can be debated but it IS the law, and all fishermen must comply.

Angling with more lines than allowed also generates many complaints from the legal fisherman who sits and watches the guy in the boat next to him doubling or tripling his chances of catching a fish. Double-lining is also a violation easily detected by patrolling game wardens.

Every so often I would get a call about a particular individual who was considered an area crappie fishing fanatic. He gave them away to his buddies at work and bragged about his fishing prowess. His mug appeared alongside a stringer of fish more than once in the local newspaper. The guy was famous for passing on tips to catch crappies. Guessing by the number of complaints, he was also known to use excessive lines in pursuing his hobby. This might help explain some of his extraordinary success.

During the winter months, it became a real challenge to witness extra lines, especially when a person was fishing inside a shelter. I knew where my "extreme" fisherman's ice house was located, but conditions were never suitable to catch him in the act. Besides, he had a watchdog. The huge, gangly mutt would lay outside the shelter door and scan the area for any intrusion; its fearsome posture appeared military-like as if it was about to warn of an approaching enemy and then strike and chew it to pieces. It was impossible to advance on this multi-lining cheater without initiating an ugly wrestling match in the snow with a dull-witted, sharp-toothed opponent. The mongrel was brought along for a specific reason, and it was doing a first-class job.

Another obstacle was the arrangement of windows on all sides of the shelter. They allowed the occupant a wide view of the entire lake, a distinct advantage if your intent is to bend the rules.

The third poaching accusation of the winter motivated me to make another stab at catching this notorious resource abuser with the goods; he was starting to rub people the wrong way.

There he was, staring at my truck as I drove by the edge of the frozen lake: the pooch from hell! My options were to walk out and warn the dog's owner (this choice would provide little deterrent in the future) or quickly devise a way to get in the shack before he had time to cut the lines. Since ticket and fine impart a more lasting effect, I chose the latter.

Four unoccupied fish houses were scattered around the lake, two of them about a hundred yards from the drooling sentinel. After hiding my patrol truck, I crept along the steep bank at the lake's edge, struggling to remain inconspicuous so as not to disturb the four-footed security guard lying 200 yards away. The deep snow allowed me to crawl to a spot along the shore opposite one of the other houses that would temporarily block the dog's view of my position.

Now what? So far, to my amazement, I hadn't been spotted. There was little hope of that continuing for the next 100-yard sprint to the neighboring shelter. I assumed an upright running position would certainly alert the hairy monster and all hell would break loose—not to mention me being seen by my suspect.

Nothing to lose now, I thought. Go for it! See if you can break the hundred-yard, full-snowmobile-suit dash. The first 20 yards were dazzling; huge strides through the snow aiming for the rear of the hut. Then he saw me! Up on all fours, the "thing" was instantly animated and appeared to be in attack mode. It began growling and snarling and gawking in my direction. Then it started to yap and bark—it was cranked!

C'mon . . . C'mon, just a few more yards until I can get out of sight behind the houses I thought as my breathing began to labor.

Just before I dived behind the house, the door opened on the target shelter and my suspect stepped out. Peaking around the corner, I couldn't believe the stroke of luck; he commenced to scream and shout at his faithful companion that was half-way to his new meal. "Get back here. Brandy, get back here now! Stay!" he yelled. The owner stepped back in the house and pulled the door behind him. Now his mutt was really distressed. Should I obey my boss's commands or assault the intruder behind the house? He must have been thinking. The dog was going nuts and wouldn't shut up. Again his master came out, looked around and told him to button up, but even a whack on the head and a gush of obscenities wouldn't subdue the critter's obsession. He wanted ME!

I now actually had a plan. This guy had violated a supreme canine decree: he wouldn't believe his own dog! It was time to take advantage of that mistake. Immediately after he re-enters the shack, I'll rush the 100 yards toward the door and hopefully shock or intimidate the creature long enough to allow me a peak into the dark interior.

If this tactic failed, perhaps my snowmobile suit would absorb the brunt of the penetrating teeth until its owner would yank his mutt off of me. A leap of faith here, but the decision had been made; I'd sacrifice my skin for a three-liner!

Here goes! Just as the door shut, my 5 pound pack boots jumped into action, carrying me through the snow-drifted surface like a galumping sea lion—not the swiftest of pursuers but good enough for a misdemeanor bust.

The toothed brute caught my advance at the 50-yard line. Two shrieking howls and we were on a collision course. It was either eat or be eaten; I ran right past him! No leaping or chewing. The yellow mass of fur just turned and followed me to the door as I jerked it open. The gawking sentry turned out to be all bark. All my angst only to discover that the keeper of the gate was a wimp!

Once inside I saw the owner go for one of the six lines with a pocket knife. He was only successful on slicing the one. After introducing myself in a wheezing voice, I moved to the center of the house blocking his access to the other holes and lines. "Now I see your technique. So this is how you manage to get the edge up on the competition!" I said with a wry inflection. (I've never been accused of being tactful or subtle.) "Whatdaya say we go outside and pet your dog!"

"I knew old Brandy was barking for some reason. Where did you come from, anyway?"

"Just out here checkin'," I said. I certainly didn't want him to think I had put out any effort.

"Nice dog you got there. Does it bite?" Slightly sarcastic, but I decided I earned that privilege on this one.

"I doubt it. Just a family pet that keeps me company."

With the niceties out of the way, I collected the bobbers, jiggle sticks and the remaining lines that he hadn't sunk, issued a summons, and continued my trek. It was a much more gratifying jaunt back to the truck!

Only two days elapsed before the word of his capture had spread around the fishing community and the plant where "Mr. Six-liner" worked.

Not that many folks were unhappy!

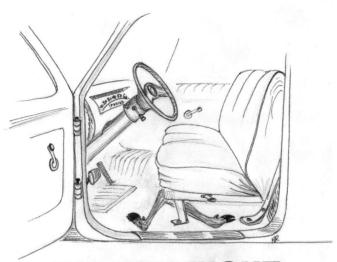

TWENTY EIGHT
The Packed Pickup

I have found illegally taken game in the most unlikely places. From fish fillets in tackle boxes to live northern pike swimming in circles in a bathtub to a fawn deer under a bed, it never ceased to amaze me where contraband could be stashed.

A great deal of deer hunting, especially on the public lands in Itasca County, consists of groups of hunters or "camps" set up at accesses or along forest roads. Tents or pickup campers are used as temporary domains for a weekend and sometimes through the duration of the season. Checking out these living quarters consumes much of an officer's patrol time.

In most cases these inspections are nothing more than a public relations effort to provide the needed visibility and deterrent necessary for good game and fish enforcement work. Also, much information about hunting conditions and success in the area is gathered here, along with an occasional cup of coffee.

Sometimes, however, there are hints that some of the folks might have stepped out of the legal bounds of the hunting rules: body language, voice inflections, or just plain direct evidence like blood and hair draw an officer's attention. One such stop along with a fellow officer provides a good example.

The camp was just shutting down late in the first Sunday afternoon of the season. All five hunters were loading equipment into their vehicles. I asked "How's the success, guys? Going home with any deer today?"

"Yeah, we got two little bucks this morning and were just ready to head south."

"I see that. Do you mind if I have a check?"

"Well, what you see is what you get. There's the two deer."

"O.K.! But if you don't mind, I'd like to check in your vehicles." It was the pause in his answer and the fact that none of them stopped their work for even a second or looked directly at us that raised my curiosity.

We checked out the first camper, finding nothing unusual. We then walked over to the other pickup with no topper. It looked as if our suspicions were wide of the mark because it was an ordinary pickup with no extended cab–an unlikely place to hide anything. Just for kicks, I reached under the seat on the passenger side and felt something furry. I bent down to look and still wasn't quite sure what was there, other than it was something covered with hair. I looked closer, and what I was touching appeared to be the white belly hair of a deer. I pulled and tugged and yanked until a whole deer literally popped out from under the seat.

This was just a normal full-size pickup with no more than nine inches of clearance between the seat and the floor. It was a small fawn that was field dressed and cold, so I assumed it was taken the day before. They had shot the fawn without a permit and somehow forced the little critter under the seat for concealment on the way home. One of the camp members admitted to the shooting and was cited; the deer was seized. I had to admit that this was the largest animal in the smallest space I had ever found–just another page in my accounts of hidden critters! It definitely taught me never to rule out the smallest hiding compartment, even if circumstances suggest otherwise.

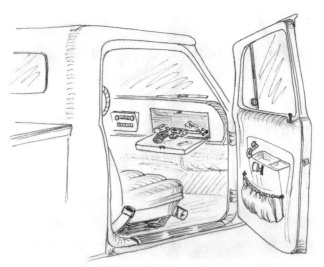

TWENTY NINE

The Disguised Surprise

Illegal spearing of spawning game fish in the spring of the year damages the future fish population of a lake due to the removal of the egg-laden females; it is also just plain unethical. Fish can became so vulnerable during this time that snatching a large walleye by hand isn't an uncommon method of taking it.

"Got your spear sharpened?" This was a retort occasionally overheard when a warden would be approached by folks who were trying to goad him. "Yeah, I heard you. Maybe I'll see you out there!" was an officer's typical rebuttal. Although done in good humor, it confirmed the past history and popularity of this spring tradition in the area. Everyone knew the locations of the many creeks that produced the big fish during the spawning run, but very few ever risked their reputations or wallets to actually partake in this prohibited method of taking fish. Yet there were a few spearers who continued to elude and frustrate enforcement for years.

The night was damp and cool, with the musky smell of the ground and the pungent breeze that always follows spring breakup. It was one of the darkest mornings I can remember, even at 1:00 A.M. The night was near black only a faint porch light a quartermile away providing any point of reference.

Lying in a depression across a narrow road from a small dam, my partner and I had been captive to the noises of spilling water, hooting owls and chirping frogs for two hours. The walleyes were big, probably the largest anywhere in the county since they were a product of the Mississippi River one mile to the south. These monster spawners would somehow find their way upstream, jump over the 2-foot spillway, and just lie there in a foot of water, defenseless to an unscrupulous fish thief.

Just after 2:00 A.M. a small, lightless pickup slowly idled to within 30 feet of us. The truck dropped off two of its occupants and then parked a quarter mile away. "Get ready. We've got activity," I whispered.

We watched the two intently as we crawled to the edge of the gravel . . . then, THUNK, the recognizable sound of metal against rock. We couldn't see it, but a spear had definitely been plunged into the water.

By crawling across the road surface, we intended to trap them on the walkway. After my partner reached the opposite end of the dam, the light from my flashlight caused the pair of poachers to dart directly into his arms shortly after a spear had been flung into the rushing depths. Both of the offenders were eventually subdued in the grass ditch beside a large, flopping walleye.

After joining up and holding a culprit in each hand, we decided to shut off our flashlights and take a short breather. I had an off-the-wall idea. "Let's see if we can capture the other two. By assisting, they're just as guilty as these boys."

After some deliberation, we came up with a strategy—we'd hide our defendants in the woods, pose as the fish poachers, and attempt to lure their partners from the hill to come pick us up. The dead-end road would force them to stop where it would be easier for us to take control. It was so dark that most likely they wouldn't recognize us until it was too late, especially if we changed our appearance to resemble these guys.

We left our lights off and carefully escorted our two cuffed bandits along the grassy ditch and into a wooded area about 50 yards from the dam. I counseled them that remaining quiet would be in their best interests. At this point they were out of sight from approaching headlights, and being handcuffed together around an elm tree, they were unable to interfere with our next plan of attack.

We removed their coats and hats and replaced them with our uniform jackets and state hats. With our clothes exchange completed, we hurried back to the dam site and picked up the spears to complete our deception.

"Go ahead and shine your light a couple times toward the pickup," I whispered. He pointed his beam up the hill and gave three short flashes. Instantly, we heard a starter engage, and the lightless vehicle began rumbling toward us. As a faint glint of the truck's bumper slowly appeared out of the blackness, brake-lights eerily reflected the whole scene until the truck made a squeaky stop within 4 feet from of our motionless outlines. Hunching over and hiding my face while running past the driver's door, I muttered through the window, "Let's get out of here, quick!" We both tossed the spears in the back and jumped in the box of the pickup!

"They'll have to turn around at the dead end. That's when we'll stop them," I said as I fumbled for the button on my flashlight. "Here we go . . . wait . . . wait . . . NOW!" Just as the truck ended its full circle turn, we engaged our lights and shoved them in the side windows hollering, "STOP THE TRUCK! GAME WARDEN!" As they slowed to a stop, we leaped from the truck, grabbed the handles and pulled the doors open revealing two extremely stunned female faces. "Please get out of the cab! We've got your partners in custody for taking fish during closed season and both of you are under arrest for assisting them."

We checked the ladies' identities and found they were the men's wives. I drove the truck the short distance back to the dam while my partner marched the women back. As he kept them under control, I uncuffed the husbands from the tree and led them to their wives.

Everyone was relaxed while their legal rights and the charges were explained until the lady passenger decided she wanted to re-enter the truck and make a call on the CB radio. She was getting more agitated by the minute, refusing to acknowledge any of our commands.

"Put the radio down. Now! Put it down!!" I could hear my partner shouting. But she continued to talk into the mike as my partner tried to pry it from her hands. She started screaming and swearing at the officer while he attempted to remove the radio transmitter.

"There. That should do it!" he said as he yanked the mike and cord out of the truck. "You won't be talking on this anymore!" We assumed she was trying to warn others in the area who were out committing the same violations.

Instead of settling down, she became more upset until we finally had to remove her from the truck and apply handcuffs. With a drunken, foreign accent, and screeching epithets into the night air, she started to scream at the top of her lungs. "I'll keel you! I'll keel you!" Standing next to the passenger door, the lady turned into a beast and was completely out of control, kicking and squealing while trying to climb back into the cab.

Helping contain her movements, I suggested to my partner that this whole crew should go to jail since she refused to cooperate and that further restraints would have to be employed on her. The others just stood there showing no willingness to help defuse their raving companion.

While my partner did his best to control the woman and keep the others in line, I searched the inside of the cab for further evidence of poaching. To this day, what I found still raises the hair on the back of both our necks. Popping open the glove compartment directly in front of where our wild lady was sitting, I removed what proved to be a loaded .38 caliber revolver!

I unloaded it and showed my partner what I found. It was too dark to see him turn ashen, but the gasps and sheer terror in his response were unmistakable.

"Wow! That thing was in there? Right in reach of this gal? I don't believe it. I think we may have dodged the big one here!!" he replied angrily. "Let's call a sheriff's squad and take them all in now. We'll force them to post a bail before being released and charge her with possession of the handgun, too!"

The case ended after all four pled guilty the following week. The entire ninety days of jail time was suspended, and small fines were assessed on each defendant, including the extra transporting loaded gun charge on the unruly woman. This whole case was another example of the court system failing to assess a large enough penalty to provide an ample deterrent. This hand-slapping outcome is the root of most frustration for game wardens. It takes many years to educate the judges and attorneys about the lethal intensity of some poachers and the threat they can be to those who get in their way.

One can only surmise about a different, and possibly more deadly, outcome to this case.

THIRTY

The Attack Deer

Game and fish road-checks have always been a good enforcement tool throughout resource agencies in the United States. It not only puts the violator on notice that a check could happen at any time while transporting unlawfully possessed animals, it also creates a big enough deterrent for many folks who may be predisposed to violating, to think twice. This in turn saves the wildlife that would otherwise be taken illegally.

When Minnesota conservation officers got the legal go-ahead to conduct road checks in the early '80s, the first contacts were overwhelmingly successful. The first large check conducted in the Deer River area involved 15 officers stopping southbound traffic on an early Saturday morning during fishing season for a three-hour period. The particular highway targeted was a junction into which many fishermen leaving cabins and resorts at the end of a week's stay were funneled. In three hours, there were 60 vehicles stopped and 59 arrests made for over-limits and other types of fishing violations. The word got out on these stops in the following years, and the rate of violations went down significantly. That's the deterrent effect!

The legal ramifications of these stops have always been scrutinized by the courts, and in 2002 a state court decision shut down the road-check practice until the appeal process was completed.

All conservation officers have stories involving bizarre discoveries while conducting game and fish road-checks. From hidden game and fish to drugs to outstanding felony warrants—you pretty much saw it all. Since the rules on conducting road-checks required that all vehicles be stopped, this technique reduced discrimination and also opened the door to the detection of violations other than game and fish.

One cool fall Sunday morning on U.S. Highway 2, a group of us were about halfway into a road-check for migratory waterfowl. Many of the cars and trucks checked were returning after a weekend of duck hunting in far northern Minnesota. Most people were pleasant and didn't mind the small inconvenience of a short stop. Many of them got out of their vehicles for a stretch and engaged us in small talk while we were conducting interviews and searches.

One particular pickup camper combination pulled up behind some cars that were getting checked out. As I approached the truck's cab, the driver jumped out and took a few steps toward me. The other passenger in the truck remained inside while I asked the driver if he had been hunting; if so, did he have any game on board? He immediately seemed nervous, and with eyes to the ground he answered, "Yes, we've been hunting in the Baudette area and have some ducks. Go ahead and look in the back." With another officer at my side, I grasped the handle on the camper door, pulled it open and instantly saw a man facing us in a sitting position. I thought the driver was nervous but nothing compared to this guy. You could see the sweat running down his temples, and his speech was almost incoherent when we asked to inspect inside the camper.

When people are put in delicate positions such as this, the humor of the moment rises to the surface. The man was in short sleeves, stuffing whole ducks into the arms of his jacket. I asked him what he was doing and he replied, "Nothing, just got these ducks here."

"Yeah, I can see the ducks, Sir, but what are you sitting on? Maybe you better jump out."

As he got up, it became very evident what he was using for a seat–the body of a large headless deer! The next obvious question to the gentleman was, "Why do you have a deer in here?" His response has to go down in the top ten of any officer's career: "We were all hunting in a blind and this deer attacked us. It was self-defense!"

I then asked him if he had any permits to cover the transportation of a big game animal or if he had called any authority to justify the possession of this animal.

The "headless" deer and an over-limit of ducks discovered during a road-check.

He said, "No, we just decided to bring it home."

"Why no head?" I asked.

"It was a buck with a large rack, and we couldn't fit the whole thing into the truck."

All three were then gathered together and told that they would be charged for transporting an illegally taken big game animal and for the possession of an over-limit of ducks.

"Also," I said, "your story of an attack deer will have to be repeated to a judge and possibly a jury if you decide to plead not guilty. Just for your information!"

The whole crew must have had a little conference before court and decided that the attack deer excuse probably would-n't hold up. They all pleaded guilty the following Monday.

THIRTY ONE

The Vicious VW

It became apparent early on in my career that harvesting spawning fish before season was a spring ritual highly anticipated among some of the resident rural population. Snatching a few illegal fish to supply a neighborhood fry or feeling the exhilaration of partaking in a prohibited sport were reasons enough to risk otherwise upstanding reputations. Many spawning creeks that meandered through backyards or public terrain were very familiar to the petty fish poacher; the logistical advantage was definitely not in favor of the local game warden.

Why I chose this particular Sunday spring morning to roam the wooded trails north of town is unclear, but I plainly remember the damp air saturated with the odors of the pre-budding hardwoods that lined the 2-mile forest road. The dawn was quiet and calm, as if the world hadn't yet risen.

Turning left off the main blacktop, I dodged the muddy holes and deep ruts, creeping deeper into the forest toward an impoundment. The icy pool fed a narrow creek that wound through thick alders and willows, and finally poured into a small lake a half mile to the east. When the spring run-off waters were plentiful, the little brook provided a brief home for small northern pike that strained to complete their upstream breeding run.

I'd had problems on this same path a year earlier. On a bright afternoon the previous spring, I parked my patrol truck and walked a mile to the creek to check water levels and signs of fish. Arriving back at my vehicle only forty minutes later, I saw that the tires had been slashed, leaving all four wheel rims on the ground.

I recalled that incident as I made my way toward the lake. Just as I rounded a mucky corner, I was startled to see a small vehicle barreling through the mire in my direction. Dirt and water blasting from all four wheels, the rusty Volkswagen continued its forward motion while I pulled over, stepped out of my truck, and signaled them to stop. With only a few yards between us now, I assumed it was going to pull up alongside me and stop. As I stood in a deep rut, it was pure habit that made me reach for the door handle. Stunned that it didn't halt, I still held on to the handle as the little car accelerated, dragging me alongside. "Hold on. Stop!" I screamed into the open window, but to no avail. The whole scene seemed surreal—the rear wheels rooster-tailing mud and I being dragged through the furrows and on past my truck!

Enough of that. Time to disengage! My hitchhiking was obviously having little effect on their intent to escape. As soon as I let loose, I felt a heavy pressure on my left thigh as the right rear tire ran over me. As I lay looking over my left shoulder, the shock of the last ten seconds came into focus—I had just been assaulted. I looked down and was amazed at my lack of injury. No broken leg. No trauma at all other than a little blood caused by the tread breaking the skin. In fact, the tread impressions were imbedded deep into the cloth of my work pants (a souvenir I kept for many years). The spongy, muddy conditions had absorbed the force and prevented a more severe injury.

I got to my feet and hobbled back to my mud-splattered truck. I climbed in and grabbed the radio mike to call for assistance. On a Sunday morning so far in the boonies, I expected little help in apprehending the three villains.

Following the Volkswagen's tracks back out, I felt if I could get to the main road quickly, I had a possibility of spotting them at the "T" intersection. When I bounced onto the tar road, I looked both ways and saw nothing due to the road's hilly contours.

I had to guess—a fifty-fifty chance of catching the offenders. I swung a hasty left. This time luck was riding with me. Just over the hill, I could see the rear of the beetle about a mile ahead. The chase was on.

Keeping dispatch aware of my location, I slammed the pedal down. A mile catch-up could take 4 or 5 miles of travel, I thought. The rear window of my target loomed larger as a few minutes passed; I continued to talk to the sheriff who was north-bound from town.

Siren blaring, I caught up with the rust-bucket on wheels sooner than I thought. I maneuvered alongside, but the driver refused to pull over. My next move included a quarter mile of grassy ditch ahead of us—a perfect resting spot for an out-of-control Bug. Cruising alongside at 60 miles per hour, I moved slowly to the right, lightly nudging the VW onto the shoulder and down into the ditch where it finally came to a rolling stop halfway up the opposite bank.

Scrambling from my patrol vehicle, I slowly approached the occupants who were still stuffed inside. "Out you come, boys," I instructed them. "And I want all your bellies lying flat on the grass." As I cautiously scrutinized each through my handgun sights, I was taken aback to see a young woman squeeze herself out from the backseat.

With all of them face down, I handcuffed the two males together while keeping my eye on the female. "O.K.! Up on your feet! Let's see what you've got!" I shouted as I checked them for weapons and other devices. One fillet knife and two pocket knives were removed from their possession.

The sheriff had now arrived and kept an eye on our suspects while I checked the interior of the vehicle. On the floor of the backseat lay a potato bag full of small northern pike. Fleeing a peace officer for a bunch of skinny fish made little sense until I popped open the glove compartment. The back of the box had been removed, allowing direct access into the hood area—and trunk—on this rear-engine car. There, its stock sticking out through the glove box, was a fully loaded 12-gauge shotgun.

Apparently, the accumulation of the two violations of transporting a loaded firearm and possession of out-of-season fish was enough, in their minds, to attempt a getaway and to assault an officer.

As usual, the court was lenient on the fish-bashing trio. A plea bargain arrangement suspended all jail time and assessed only minor fines for each. Resisting arrest, assaulting an officer, transporting a loaded gun and possession of fish out of season were all bargained down to a year probation and a $500 total fine. Because of limited time, and in some cases, judicial disinterest, it is difficult to explain to a judge the harrowing experiences that led to these arrests. This wasn't the first time a feeling of dejection and resentment for the system had enveloped me, but as officers, we are taught our job is only to bring them in—not seek to be judge and jury.

Sometimes an attitude prevails among judges in the criminal justice system that dangerous and fear-provoking situations are expected as part of an officer's duties. To a certain extent, this may be. But a stiffer penalty for those perpetrators who choose this behavior would certainly provide added satisfaction to the officers who risk injury and death to protect the public's natural resources. A warden never knows what awaits him while on patrol, even if it's on an obscure trail in the woods on a mild April morning.

Officer Chapin's patrol vehicle after all four tires were slashed.

THIRTY TWO
The Corroborating Candy Wrapper

A conservation officer's job is sprinkled with periods of frustrations, but no greater than when the results of illegal deeds are unearthed and you know from your experiences that all the investigation in the world won't lead to the capture of the game thieves. It's especially disturbing when animals are found decomposing or aren't retrieved. This is one of the top issues that repulses the nonhunting public and reduces the legal hunter's integrity.

There should be a significant penalty for the wasting of meat or the wasting of an animal. People who do this should not be classified as hunters and they should have their hunting privileges removed for a long time. But that's the court's job, and so far these types of violations are only misdemeanors.

Back when antlerless deer permits were hard to get, or not even issued in some areas, many fawns and does were shot and left in the woods. It's irresponsible enough to shoot something that you can't identify, but to not report the mistake just compounds the crime.

Most officers tend toward leniency when a hunter reports he has accidentally killed illegal game, if for no other reason than to guarantee salvaging the animal.

While working the first morning of one of the warmer deer openers, a fellow officer and I received a call about 9:00 A.M. that a hunter in Balsam Township had discovered two deer near a stand that he was going to use. Upon arrival, we spotted the caller next to his vehicle, and he then guided us to the site about one-quarter mile off the trail.

There, about 100 feet apart and 40 yards from a deer stand, were two adult doe deer lying dead. Each had been taken with one shot. They also appeared to be unsalvageable due to the decomposition in the unusually high temperature. After questioning the caller and being satisfied that he had nothing to do with this, we dragged the two animals to our truck and loaded them in the box. This seemed to be another one of those cases, with no witnesses, to be put on the cold case list—just about impossible to make! There were many hunters in the area, but with nothing to go on, interviews would have been a waste of time, especially with all the other obligations we had that day.

One of the deer still had a slug under its skin, which appeared to be 30-caliber. Throwing that in the ashtray, we continued with our many duties and checked several hunters on the way out. Discussing this case with my partner that evening, we both came to the same conclusion: we needed to see if we could come up with more evidence that might lead us to something. We both hated this type of resource waste abuse, and we couldn't get this case out of our minds.

By early the next morning we had developed a plan. Might there be shell casings near or even under the deer stand, and if so, might they match a firearm belonging to a hunter still in the vicinity? Using a metal detector borrowed from a sporting-goods store, we took turns circling the ground around the deer stand until we discovered two shell casings within a foot of each other, both .308 caliber! We also found a small Snickers candy wrapper directly under the platform.

Immediately we drove to the nearest camp and started to interview the hunters as they returned to their tents after the morning hunt. We found out that there were nine hunters in the group. Eight of them returned to the site by noon, and all firearms were checked as they entered camp. None of them had a .308 rifle. The whole group cooperated enthusiastically. They also were repulsed by shooting deer and leaving them to rot.

I asked one of the party members where the ninth person in the group might be, and he said that Bill went home the night before due to an illness. (Later we discovered that Bill faked his illness to his hunting buddies.) Further inquiry revealed that Bill hunted with an old lever action .308 with black tape wrapped around the handle and that, yes, he liked miniature Snickers candy bars. Finally I learned that Bill lived in the suburbs of the Twin Cities. After getting Bill's full name and finding a phone book, we were out of there and on our way to the Twin Cities, 200 miles away.

Arriving at the residence after dark and in a light snowstorm, I knocked on Bill's door and waited. A middle-aged man opened the door and greeted us with, "What's up?" We identified ourselves as he stepped outside in his stocking feet and pulled the door closed behind him. We told him that we were investigating the taking and wasting of two doe deer in Itasca County and asked if he had been hunting yesterday in that area and if he knew anything about this situation. Bill immediately admitted that he was hunting there but denied any knowledge about the two does.

I sneaked a glance at my partner and we both nodded slightly, realizing that Bill was lying. His body language and his closing the door behind him confirmed our suspicions of his guilt. Our plan was to get him to confess within our rules of enforcement procedure. No Miranda warning was required because he was not in custody and could leave or stop talking at any time. We told him that. We asked if he would like to put some shoes on or if we could talk inside, but he said no to that idea, probably due to his wife being inside.

As we continued to ask questions of Bill, we both slowly drew back to the middle lawn area where there was an inch of snow. Mr. Bill followed us slowly and continued to deny the charges even while standing in the snow in his stocking feet. After about twenty minutes questioning Bill as the freezing snow covered his feet, I hit him with the evidence of the .308 shells, the Snickers bars, and a tape-handled rifle. "If we could just see the rifle you used up north, we could clear this thing up and be out of here," I said.

Bill refused to show us his gun and didn't want to go back in and tell his wife what was happening, so after freezing for half an hour between the law and his fireplace, good old Bill admitted that he had made a mistake and had shot the deer in question.

I thanked him for finally coming through with the truth, but one more thing I needed to see was the taped gun. He went in and brought it out and it was immediately seized for evidence (and eventually confiscated.) Bill appeared in court and pleaded guilty.

Bill didn't let us in on the reason he shot and then wasted two beautiful animals. If he didn't know what he was shooting at, he certainly should have. Was he overwhelmed by the moment? It's obvious he wasn't a seasoned poacher since the meat wasn't taken! The senselessness of crimes like Bill's is not always understood. Studies have shown that all hunters go through stages as they mature through the years. The phases start at the Shooter stage, then progress to the Limit, Trophy, Method and finally the Sportsman stage. I think Bill never emerged from the Shooter stage!

Diligence, persistence, whatever it takes—a conservation officer has to sometimes go by the seat of his pants when the evidence isn't staring him in the face. We felt good on the way home. The case that couldn't be made!

Here are the two large does found below a deer stand and left to rot.

THIRTY THREE
The Brazen Trio

Skimming full speed across the slightly rippled surface of a large lake in a powerful boat was a special delight, especially on a beautiful, clear 70-degree day. Lake Winnibigoshish afforded me many hours of extraordinary beauty and fulfillment while making the rounds for illegal fishing activity. From time to time, I'd have to remind myself that I was getting paid for this awful drudgery.

The absolute best part of the job was visiting people in a recreational setting. For many, it was their only opportunity to "go north" for the summer and fully relax. My enjoyment came from sharing fishing experiences, personal events and answering questions of the whereabouts of existing hotspots. We were supposed to know all these things. Almost everyone was upbeat and courteous while their licenses and fish were being inspected–most folks having never been checked by a game warden.

It was the third consecutive gorgeous day and the walleyes were hungry! Two hours of patrolling brought me to the west side of the big lake where hundreds of boats were scattered in groups along the five-mile shoreline. Everyone seemed to be catching fish at a decent rate, so it was time to survey a cluster of 35 boats at a distance.

Occasionally an officer can increase his odds of spotting potential infractions by lying back for a moment and studying body language. Sometimes a dishonest fisherman will provide a clue as to his intentions. A particular turn of the head, the rate of casts, scanning of the horizon, distance from other boats, number of lines—clues like these may suggest deceptive behavior. Since examining every boat is impractical, it just makes sense to employ a bit of intuition drawn from years of checking thousands and thousands of fishermen.

This setting hadn't exposed any of the usual indications that would lead me to approach a suspect boat. I just pulled into the crowd and randomly chose a shiny green, low-profile 18-footer occupied by three men casting and trolling.

"How ya doin', guys? Conservation Officer. Just like to take a quick look at your licenses and fish. We'll just pull up alongside." My civilian partner held onto the gunwales as I leaned over and inspected the documents.

"I see you're all from Wisconsin. How are you all doing on fish? Close to your limit yet?" A muttered response from all three forced me to repeat the question.

"I think we have close to our limit," mumbled the operator, as I watched the reactions of the other two. They had none. No expressions. They continued to work their reels as I handed back the licenses. I inquired as to which of the two live-wells contained their fish.

"They're all in that one," said the driver as he pointed to the one on my side.

Since he was not about to assist me, I reached over and popped the cover open. I could see bunches of fish swirling around in the dark greenish water.

"How many you got here?" I repeated.

The same answer came back, "Probably a limit." It was expressed with such little conviction that it forced me to jump in the boat and physically remove each fish for a full count—two under the limit. Any more fish anywhere?"

"Nope. That's about it!"

"How about this other live-well?" There was no reply—just quiet indifference. I opened the hinged door and "surprise"— another container full of walleyes!

"Appears like you're all a few over. I'll take a look at your licenses and I.D.'s again after I make a total count. Why don't you all remain seated!"

The final tally came to 35—almost double the daily limit. Because of their nonresident status, I was obliged to collect bail money prior to releasing them. A court appearance would not be required if they chose to forfeit the bail.

The boat's owner coughed up the money for all three. He handed me eleven of the eighteen $100 bills in his wallet; it looked as if he carried a cache of currency just in case something like this happened! The casual attitude that all three projected was puzzling. It was as if the whole encounter was a joke and no big deal. Smiling and laughing, one of them asked if they could continue fishing the next day. I explained that it was legal to take a limit of fish the following day since their fishing licenses could not be revoked for this type of violation. (This has changed since 2002.)

After collecting all the fish and pushing off, I retained a skeptical feeling about the whole crew; I just had a sense of something not quite right. I made up my mind I wasn't through with them!

There were many more boats to single out, although some had left after they had witnessed our encounter. But instead of continuing to check, I motored in the opposite direction and slowed to a stop about a mile north. While I peered through my binoculars, the suspicious boat had roared off toward a public access ten miles away, its wake leaving a trail like a compass needle. "We're going to follow them," I said to my partner.

The next twenty minutes led us across the widest expanse of Winni to a well-known launching site on the east shore. The instant I saw them idle up to the dock, I steered our craft to the north and at full speed headed for my truck. My intentions were to get back to my pickup as fast as possible and drive 5 miles south to intercept the trio at a major intersection. At this point I would follow behind hopefully undetected and track them back to their cabin or motel.

The timing was perfect! Just as we approached the junction on the state highway, I could see them pull out ahead of us. They were south, so we tagged along at a safe distance behind. At the little town of Deer River, they proceeded east toward Grand Rapids. Once in town, the pickup and attached boat and trailer headed south directly into a motel parking lot.

Having called for assistance during the 30-mile trip, I radioed my suspicions to a fellow officer; they most likely had more fish in their room!

As soon as we saw them park, I put on a cover-jacket and ran into the lobby from where I continued to track them down a hallway to a room door.

Just when the third party was entering the room, I ran to the door and inserted my foot between it and the frame. "Hi, it's me again. Just had one more question," I said to the dumbfounded guest. "Mind if I step in for a minute? By this time, my partner had arrived on the scene and added to the enforcement presence.

"Yeah. Sure. Come in. I thought everything was taken care of."

"Since this is your third day here from Wisconsin, we presume you have more fish than what you showed us in the boat. . . . What do you have in the cooler over there? Can we look?"

"Just some food and a couple fillets for dinner."

"O.K.! Let's see what you've got." Lying in the container packed with ice was a mass of unpackaged walleye fillets—another 16 fish to add to the previous numbers.

Come to find out, this was the second of three trips to Minnesota the group planned for this year. They also admitted this was their seventh year fishing the big lake. We amended the three summonses to fit the extra over-limit and collected another $200 in bail—an added penalty that would hopefully provide a deterrent for future violations.

The arrogance and selfishness exhibited by these fish thieves suggests that education may be the only way to reduce the overwhelming desire to pig out on fish and ignore the law. Lessons in fish management, fairness and ethics might do more than large fines, license revocation or equipment confiscation.

The lesson I learned from this is that if all you have is a hunch, a gut feeling, or a sixth sense (or whatever handle you attach to it), allow your intuition and instincts to guide your way.

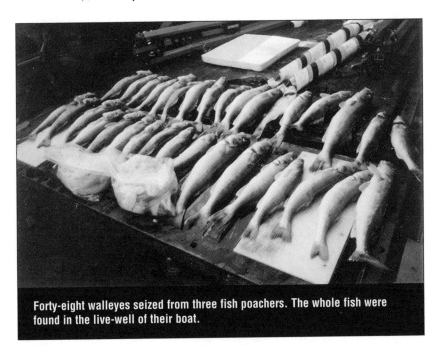

Forty-eight walleyes seized from three fish poachers. The whole fish were found in the live-well of their boat.

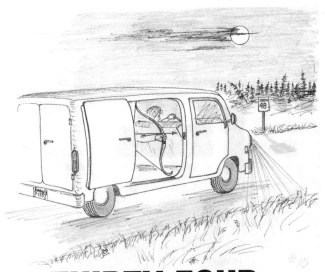

THIRTY FOUR
The Slow-Speed Follow

The act of shining an artificial light at an animal in order to temporarily halt its movement, and then shooting it, has been illegal for a century in this country. In fact, records go back as far as the mid-1800s in some states declaring "shining" off limits while hunting. The proper or ethical way to take a deer, or any animal for that matter, is determined by the historical traditions and customs of a particular society. This "fair chase" is mostly in the eyes of the beholder and is molded as a behavior through current laws as one grows into a mature hunter.

Minnesota declares the shining of any wild animal as a major offense and classifies it as a gross misdemeanor. The only exception to shining is when hunting raccoons, where a light may be used to take the animal, once it has been treed with the aid of dogs. This exemption is an example of a tradition that has been handed down for centuries and is reflected in the current law.

Minnesota game wardens and conservation officers have devoted many of their working hours trying to catch deer shiners in their patrol areas, not only to save some animals for the legal hunters, but also to reduce the horrendously unsafe practice of night shooting.

The '70s and '80s in Itasca County were no exception to this type of illegal behavior. Working all hours of the night trying to nab these people was tiring and dangerous, but also exciting. The poachers' loaded guns and, in most cases, their use of alcohol, combined to make every stop a tactical surprise. A prerequisite for success when working deer shiners was choosing a surveillance position that provided the greatest chance of the deer and violator coming together, and most important, where the officer could observe the final act of shining. This required a good amount of planning and knowledge of the roads and fields, of which Itasca County has plenty. A typical shiner would travel miles throughout the county drifting from field to field using either a handheld spotlight or the headlights of the car. Some were smarter than others in avoiding detection.

In the mid-'80s, I was patrolling at 1:30 A.M. an area north of Grand Rapids notorious for shining activity. I had had success on these roads before, and this particular night was an overcast, drizzly evening—perfect for deer movement and reduced detection. With me was a civilian partner who had ridden with me before and could be counted on for assistance. Parked and hidden just off a small county road on a forest trail, we had only been stationary for about fifteen minutes when a van was observed slowly traveling east past our unit. At this time in the morning and with no residence either way for four miles, this van got our attention. It was a very dark, moonless night, so following this vehicle required no headlights, only the use of a low-level light mounted on the front bumper. This small light illuminated the road in front of us for about 30 feet, but was almost undetectable to anyone ahead of us. With the help of the taillights from the vehicle being followed and this "sneak" light, a car can be tracked safely up to about 30 miles per hour. We tagged along about 100 feet behind the van for the next eight miles, never exceeding 25 miles per hour. This slow speed was another hint that spotting a deer was probably an objective here. We followed the van out onto a blacktop county road, around the gas pumps of a darkened store lot and then back the same way we came. All this time, a spotlight was never observed, although it appeared that the right headlight was out of alignment, shining slightly into the ditch.

The next 12 miles were no more exciting than the previous, still traveling at no more than 25 miles per hour. Then, brake lights! The van slowly came to a stop with our truck 50 feet behind. A shadowy figure emerged from the right side of the van with a bow and arrow in hand. It was difficult under the light conditions to see exactly what happened next, but a deer jumped across the ditch and into a field, first passing in front of the van's headlights. The dark silhouette of the person then re-entered the van and continued driving in the same direction. I marked the side of the road with a foot scratch in the dirt and continued to follow.

This went on for another 9 miles, when suddenly I saw a large buck on the side of the road and the van's brake lights come on again. Apparently the van saw it, too. It continued to slow down for the next quarter mile, then gradually turned around in the middle of the road. Now there was only one choice. We had to stop it. As it turned enough to shine its lights on our vehicle, I stopped within 20 feet of its bumper, hit the red lights and ran to the right side of the van. The large door on the side of the van was open, and my flashlight illuminated a person struggling to get a bow in a case while arrows were flying all over the inside of the compartment. Identifying myself, I ordered the individual to step out, and at the same time advised the female driver to stay put. She wouldn't turn off the motor as ordered, so I was forced to reach in and remove the keys. Getting both people out in front of the headlights, I confirmed their identities, and because of the equipment observed, told them they were both under arrest for shining deer. The van, the bow, and the arrows were seized for evidence and the parties were told they would be notified of a future first appearance court date.

That was the arrest. Now some interesting follow-up in this case. This probably wasn't the first time this husband-and-wife poaching team tried to use an illegal method to take a deer.

Further checking revealed that this hunter had done very well in the local big buck archery contests. One has to rethink the validity of some of these contest winners, considering this was the second shining case with a bow and arrow that I had witnessed in three years where the violator had just purchased a big buck contest ticket.

Assuming that these two people were most likely to plead not guilty, it was now important to put a first-rate effort into gathering evidence for a probable court case. The next morning, I went to the site where I had marked the road after I witnessed the defendant outside of the van with his bow. I assume he shot at the deer, but there would be no proof unless I could find an arrow that matched the same arrows that we seized.

An hour later, with the help of a metal detector, there it was, lying in the deep grass about 40 yards off the road. The arrow was a complete match to those on the bow's quiver we had seized. Our next step was to take a look at the van's lighting system. Mounted on the front right bumper was a fog light slanted at a 45-degree angle toward the ditch. That explained what I saw the night before when it appeared from the rear that one of the headlights was out of symmetry. We could not find a switch for this fog light and couldn't figure out how to turn it on or if it even functioned, until we followed the wiring back into the passenger compartment. A little ingenuity by Mr. Poacher revealed a wire attached to the high-beam switch on the floor. It allowed him to utilize the shining light only when his high-beam switch was on. This would reduce detection from approaching vehicles by just switching to low-beam. Also, there was a makeshift bench mounted inside the large sliding door so the poacher could sit and look to the side and actually shoot the bow from inside the vehicle.

With all these bits of evidence, it was now time to face a jury. Both husband and wife would be tried together, and the county attorney gave us thumbs up on quick convictions. After all, the evidence was pretty much overwhelming as to intent, plus I had a witness who would testify to everything I observed.

The trial lasted two days. The defense tactic was complete and total fabrication. For instance, Mr. Poacher's elderly father, who was permanently confined to a wheelchair, was pushed to a position directly in front of the jury. He testified that he was the installer of the fog light in the van. This was for safety purposes so his son would have better visibility to and from his rural home. The problem was, the father was also totally blind; quite a feat for such an intricate wiring job!

Mr. Poacher testified that the reason for the side-mounted sofa-type seat in the van was due to his chronic back problem. This was the only position he could ride comfortably. He also testified that he was in no condition to even pull a bow (equipped with a night-sight) and demonstrated his inability in front of the jury.

His wife just liked to go out and look at deer with her husband and had no intent on taking one. Her choice of tacky, somewhat revealing attire, and overly applied makeup was a little obvious. "I couldn't be a mean old poacher who kills animals," she was implying.

The sympathy path was getting deeper, and I was wondering if there was any way to stop it. I said to myself, Just look at the jury, give the facts, and they will do their job. Stick to the basics. Finally, after all the witnesses' testimonies and final statements, the jury went out at 3:00 P.M. I went home and told the bailiff to call me when the jury came back.

At 5:30 P.M. it was the judge himself who called. He had spent the last two hours growing more infuriated with the tactics and obvious lies by the defendants and wanted me to be there when the verdict was read. He said, "When these two are found guilty, I plan on giving them the maximum sentence. These are some seasoned poachers, and we're going to send a message in this county."

Maximum sentence was a $3,000 fine and a year in jail. As I sat in court and the jury filed in, I thought, This is what this job is all about—justice, and keeping things fair out there for the average sportsmen who buy licenses and expect others to abide by the same laws to which they are bound.

NOT GUILTY! Did I hear that right? Both defendants were found not guilty of the crime of shining; an unexpected result for sure, but more like a major disappointment. No, an officer shouldn't get so personally involved with his cases; professionalism should take the lead. But game and fish cases are so tough to make. However, this is the process and we accept it with all the frustrations.

The judge motioned me to meet him in chambers. As I opened the door to his office, I saw him remove his robe and throw it into the corner behind his desk. If the judge was that upset, I guess I also had a little right. I actually felt better! His Honor told me, "It's been a long time since I've seen such a disregard for the justice system by a couple of liars like that! I really was going to send a message." He also later admonished the current jury pool who had found the last 29 out of 30 defendants not guilty.

The next night I was out there again! I was a little discouraged, but that wore off as soon as I took in the smell of the night air, the ghostly images of the trees, and the mystery of what might materialize next.

This is the arrow found in the field. "I shot an arrow into the air, and where it fell the warden knows where!"

THIRTY FIVE
The Alien Impostor

T he law enforcement community may not hold the record
for practical jokes played on each other, but I doubt there
are many "brotherhoods" who can compete with the
degree of cunning and resourcefulness an officer will invest to
humiliate a fellow co-worker. You would think a bunch of people
who carry guns for a living might be inclined to restrain themselves from creating havoc amongst the troops. Not the case if
you wore a badge; it was open season—anytime, anywhere!
Nothing was sacred.

A few notable examples of prankster amusement have been
fixed in my mind forever. How about my neighboring officer,
for example, arriving home after a three-day trip and being
unable to locate his personal car in the airport lot . . . because
an attorney friend had it painted pink in his absence.

Or a fellow worker setting me up at a spearing creek on a
late spring evening. I stealthily approached the water's edge
only to see a dark human figure running hastily from the scene.
Of course I gave chase, bursting out of the alder brush onto a
hay field and up over a hill to get within four feet of the fleet-

footed suspect. Instantly he turned around. "Just wanted to see if you still had it in ya," blurted my working partner hysterically.

Or the day I told a local police officer friend that I had a car-kill deer for sale. He could meet me at a gas station where the deer could be transferred to his vehicle. Actually, the animal lying on my backseat was being taken to a vet following its removal from the Mississippi River where it had fallen through the ice. Its feet were bound but it was quite alive! Officer Dave was a great guy and a good friend . . . which is probably why our relationship survived.

Just before Dave drove up to the gas station, I had gathered five spectators together who now were peering through the large station window. "How come you put the deer in your backseat?" Dave asked.

"No room in the trunk. Go ahead and throw it in your squad. I'm going inside to do the paperwork."

As the six of us spied through the glass awaiting the inevitable, Dave opened the sedan's rear door and coolly grabbed the expected "dead" critter. In an instant, the doe's head snapped up from the seat, and with a loud bawl, the 150 pounds of taut sinew lunged forward, attempting to free itself from its leg restraints. Both of Dave's arms shot skyward while he took two huge jumps backwards. Utterly disoriented, the reverse stagger caused his hat to be blown off where it rolled end over end to the base of the gas pumps. Scores of expletives were muffled by the thick glass; however, my name was one thing that could be easily identified among his sputterings.

After retrieving his cap and waving universal hand signals in our direction, Dave jumped in his police car and spun out of the lot barely missing two approaching vehicles on the crowded street. "This is what good friends are all about," I proudly expressed to my fellow observers, all of whom were still out of control with laughter.

I always considered this next gag my favorite for two reasons: it wasn't done to me, and it took advantage of a couple of my closest enforcement buddies. What better reasons!

You have to understand the professionalism and authoritativeness exuded from these two members of the State Patrol to fully appreciate the situation. Loyal and hard working, they took immaculate care of their sparkling patrol cars. These guys were the epitome of perfection with their spit-shined boots, spotless uniforms and perfectly positioned Mountie hats; they were troopers at their finest.

They were also very serious. Known as the "Write Brothers," this partnership in fighting corruption wrote up record DWI arrest totals. No messing around with these boys; they were all business.

The call came over the radio one early fall evening. "I'm not sure what it is. The driver said the thing jumped out in front of him and he couldn't avoid smacking it. I'll meet you at the scene . . . two miles east on Highway 2."

Warden Woody and I were monitoring this transmission from one of the "Write Brothers" while we sipped coffee in my home office. "I don't have any idea what it is," continued my State Patrol buddy. "It's black and about three feet in length with a long tail."

"I'm about a minute away. Between the two of us, we'll figure out what it is," reflected the second "Write Brother."

A few minutes later, the sheriff's office, who were also listening, asked the two officers if they had the animal identified yet.

"No. Don't know what it could be. It's not a raccoon . . . why don't you give Tom a call and see if he's home. We can bring it over there for him to look at."

Woody and I looked at each other as if we were reading each other's minds and nodded in agreement. It just had to be done!! Circumstances and timing couldn't have been more perfect to perpetrate a devious little scheme on our two "enforcement brothers." We knew exactly what the animal in question was. They had perfectly described a fisher: a large, dark American arboreal carnivorous fur-bearing mammal related to the weasels.

"Woody, grab the animal book next to you. Let's see what could be substituted for a fisher." Quickly we leafed through the pictured pages. "There . . . perfect!" I said as I pointed to a similarly sized animal with a long tail. "Cacomistle: a carnivore related to and resembling the raccoon. Inhabits northern Mexico and far southwestern United States. This'll work. Let's get the story down before they call. I'll casually identify it as a cacomistle; a young female due to the lack of rings on its tail . . . and you come along and back me up. Sound good?"

"Yeah . . . that should work," Woody mused as the phone rang.

"Tom . . . Sheriff's office. Couple patrol boys have a critter they can't identify. Could you help 'em out? They said they'd be right over."

"You bet . . . we'll be waiting."

The two shiny maroon patrol vehicles pulled into the driveway as the first uniformed officer popped his trunk.

"Hi, boys. Whatdaya got?"

"Just picked some furry thing off the highway about the size of a big skunk. Maybe you could tell us what it is and if it might be protected."

Pulling the creature out of the trunk and laying it on the blacktop, I routinely said, "Oh, you've got a cacomistle here. Haven't seen one of these in a while. They normally only reside as far north as southern Minnesota . . . somewhat unusual in this area. What do you think, Woody?"

Woody couldn't have done a better job if he had gone to acting school. "Yup, that's what it is alright. I've seen a couple in the last few years. Looks like a young female, too—no rings on the tail!"

"Are you positive?" questioned my maroon-clad buddy.

"Well sure. Look at the nose . . . only one animal that ugly around here . . . they're protected too . . . like the mountain lion!"

"Never heard of one of these . . . " voiced the second soon-to-be deceived road cop. "What did you say it was again?"

"Cacomistle . . . C-a-c-o-m-i-s-t-l-e. Like I say, not many around . . . fairly rare! I'll probably take it to the local college for use as a mounted display."

"Cacomistle . . . hmm . . . never heard . . . well . . . O.K . . . first time I've ever seen one," muttered our first victim, still reluctant to accept my professional verdict.

Woody now filled in the gaps to finish them off. "Well, boys," he said, "this is so much smaller than the one I found last year near Aitkin. Good sign to see them reproducing in the area." We could hear the final swallow. The bait had been taken, and we had successfully set the hooks!

The drama continued the next day as the word got around the cop watering-holes that a cacomistle had been found by none other than the "Write Brothers." Ironically, they were the chief promoters of the joke on themselves. The entire law enforcement community was soon in on our cruel caper . . . everyone extolling the highly prized cacomistle as the find of the year. The cacomistle became an accepted inhabitant of Itasca County!

A week was my limit. It was time to face the music and reveal the horrid hoax to our gluttons of gullibility.

The timing was ideal . . . afternoon cop coffee break . . . all law enforcement departments present for the unveiling. "Hey, trooper guys . . . Ya ever hear of a fisher?"

"Well . . . yes. Never seen one, though. Why?"

"Just thought you would want to know I made an awful mistake on that animal you brought over the other night . . . it wasn't a cacomistle . . . just a plain ole fisher. Hope I didn't cause you guys too much awkwardness. Thought you should know." All heads turned toward the two victims in humorous anticipation. Seconds later, four cold steely eyes sliced in my direction through the tense air. Their usual cheerful moods and smiley grins turned into serious scowls.

I thought it a good time to leave as I threw a buck down for the coffee and cruised out the door. Later, I heard lots of rumors about the conversations that took place following my exit, but who listens to rumors; they couldn't have possibly known all those things about my ancestry and personal habits. I did, however, make it a point to be very alert for a time until things settled down. During subsequent conversations, they always mentioned "owing me something." So far I've never collected!

About the Author

Tom Chapin is a native of Hibbing, Minnesota. He earned his bachelor's degree in zoology in 1972 from the University of Minnesota, Duluth, after a two-year tour in the U.S. Army. Most of his twenty-nine year career as a natural resource conservation officer has been spent in the Grand Rapids, Minnesota, district where he also served as Area Supervisor for seven years. Chief among the honors he has received include the 1978 "Itasca County Law Enforcement Officer of the Year" and the 1985 "Minnesota Conservation Officer of the Year." Chapin has also served as Adjunct Faculty, teaching law enforcement courses at Itasca and Hibbing Community Colleges. Recently, the author's campaigning and testimony prompted the Minnesota State Legislature to enact a gross over-limit law. Known as the "Chapin Bill," this law became effective March 1, 2003. It increases penalties, including the loss of hunting and fishing privileges, for violators who take large quantities of game and fish.

Throughout his career as a game warden, Chapin took hundreds of photographs documenting illegal activities. These photos, many of which are included here, were an integral part of Chapin's group presentations which have both educated and entertained audiences interested in natural resources issues. Tom and his wife Sandy raised daughters Colleen, Anita, and Beth in Grand Rapids where he has recently retired from public service.